Benchmarking: Focus on World-Class Practices

Published by
AT&T Quality Steering Committee

For more information about consulting services
and training in the methods and tools
described in this book, contact the
AT&T Quality Helpline at **1-908-204-1099**

Order additional copies by select code 500-454 from:

AT&T's Customer Information Center
Order Entry Department
P.O. Box 19901
Indianapolis, IN 46219
1-800-432-6600

Developed by the AT&T Benchmarking Team
Edited and produced by the AT&T Bell Laboratories Technical Publications Center

AT&T Quality Policy

Quality excellence is the foundation for the management of our business and the keystone of our goal of customer satisfaction. It is, therefore, our policy to:

- Consistently provide products and services that meet the quality expectations of our customers.

- Actively pursue ever-improving quality through programs that enable each employee to do his or her job right the first time.

Robert E. Allen

Robert E. Allen
Chairman of the Board and Chief Executive Officer

Preface

Benchmarking is gaining momentum in U.S. corporations as a process that encourages an external focus on best practices. As a technique for developing valuable information and insights, benchmarking complements AT&T's other quality management methods and tools for implementing a Total Quality Approach.

The AT&T Benchmarking Team developed this book about benchmarking for the AT&T Quality Steering Committee and Corporate Quality Office. The AT&T Benchmarking Team is a consortium of internal AT&T benchmarking service providers. The team integrated their successful approaches and techniques to develop a systematic AT&T benchmarking process that serves as the foundation of the book.

The development of this book provided opportunities for networking among benchmarking service suppliers, and customers and potential customers of benchmarking services throughout the corporation. This involvement and participation have enhanced AT&T's overall understanding and implementation of the benchmarking process and highlighted the continuing need to keep customers actively involved during each phase of any development process.

AT&T Quality Steering Committee

Corporate Quality Office

Acknowledgments

Orchestrated teamwork across business units and divisions throughout AT&T encouraged communication among suppliers, customers, and potential customers of benchmarking within the corporation and enabled the creation of this AT&T Quality Library book. We greatly acknowledge that teamwork.

We appreciate the invaluable direction, leadership, and support that Hosein Fallah provided from the outset of this project. We thank Tom Bean and Andy Gerigk for enabling this partnership to achieve mutual goals by empowering and supporting us throughout the process. We thank Jeff Hooper for Corporate Quality Office support.

The AT&T Benchmarking Team agreed upon a unified AT&T benchmarking process, partnered to achieve supplier cooperation, and reviewed this book. In addition to ourselves, members included:

Katy Badt	Bernie English	Darel Hull
Tom Bean	Hosein Fallah	Marcie Mann-Clark
Gordy Buchanan	Jeanne Fisher	Janet Sheppard
Steve Byland	Andrew Gerigk	Ron Sucher
Debbie Chaskin	Jacques Gros	Kam Yeung

We especially thank Bob Camp, of Xerox, for his pioneering work in benchmarking; Carol Catalano for providing overall project management support that far exceeded our expectations; Brenda Klafter and Dennis Percher for reviewing the book and clarifying sub-activities within the process developed by the AT&T Benchmarking Team; and Jane Redfern for her dedication to quality, keeping us focused, and reviewing this book.

Thanks to the Benchmarking Sharing Rally participants and the following individuals who participated in customer interviews and sub-teams based on their business planning, quality, and benchmarking experiences:

Joan Ardizzone	Bill Hauser	Bill Scheerer
Surinder Chadha	John Hendrick	Laurie Seese
Elaine Chancer	Judy Horsfield	Howie Singer
Debbie Chaskin	Sharon Inger	Paul Vassil
Beth Ercolino	Debbie Lautenbach	Randall Willie
Margaret Ervin-Willis	Joe Malecki	Dick Wilson
Al Giraldi	Lynnell Murphy	Rick Wright
Bruce Gundaker	Don Padilla	Janet Yaple

George Tucker guided us well in preparing our project plan, allowed us use of his office (and coffee maker) and sustained our senses of humor.

Thanks to Sue Serritella, our editor, and to the Bell Labs Technical Publication Center team who helped to develop and produce this book: Susan Annitto, Maureen Clune, Peggy Dellinger, Pat McGinn, Kim Snow, and Marilyn Tomaino.

We applaud our reviewers who expended time to provide us with insightful and constructive comments, greatly improving the final version of the book:

Susan Bailey	Sharon Kettyle	Arthur Soderberg
Clarence Biggs	Rudy Krejci	Barbara Spiegel
Daniel Bracciale	Dan Krupka	Art Stadlin
Robert Breen	Larry Lafaro	Don Still
Leslie Brewer	Dave Lewinski	Marcia Straub
Luis Castillo	Lynnell Murphy	Joe Timmons
Surinder Chadha	Barbara Nevar-Olsen	Debbie Watson
Elaine Chancer	Jan Norton	Becky Wells
Charlie Davis	Makiko Parsons	Lisa Whitney
Susan Denney	Frank Politano	Randall Willie
Rudy Drechsler	Chris Rapposelli-Manzo	Ed Wirth
Bruce Gundaker	LuAnn Schaffernoth	Joe Wolzansky
Howard Helms	Dave Setzer	Alfred Wyche
Genie Herrington	Howard Singer	Janet Yaple

Kathleen Mallette

Kathleen Mallette

Joanne Tomlinson

Joanne Tomlinson

AT&T Benchmarking Team

Contents

About This Book

Purpose

This book introduces a common language and understanding of benchmarking across AT&T, using the best practices available today. This book is a useful benchmarking reference tool. It

- Shows how benchmarking fits into a total quality management system.

- Highlights AT&T experiences in benchmarking.

- Recommends a benchmarking process.

- Enables significant process improvements through the use of proven benchmarking techniques.

Audience

This book addresses two audiences: benchmarking planners and benchmarking participants.

Planners include senior management, strategic planners, business planners, quality planners, operational planners, and any others who might decide when to initiate a benchmarking activity. Participants include the benchmarking sponsor, process owners, quality consultants, team leaders, team members, and stakeholders involved in actually implementing the benchmarking process.

How to use this book

This book is divided into two parts to serve as a useful guide for all participants in a benchmarking activity. Part I, Supporting a Total Quality Approach, positions benchmarking in the business planning process and describes its role in the context of process management. Part II details the nine-step AT&T Benchmarking Process. An appendix includes useful references, AT&T case studies, templates, and checklists. The back cover foldout summarizes the inputs, outputs, and checkpoint activities required for each step of the AT&T Benchmarking Process.

Those who initiate and participate in the benchmarking activity will look to particular sections of Part II to lead them through their specific responsibilities in the benchmarking effort. The following table lists the chapters participants should find most useful for their roles.

Participants	Part I	Chapter 1	2	3	4	5	6	7	8	9
Planners	■	■					■	■		■
Decision makers	■	■					■	■		■
Benchmarking team			■	■	■	■	■	■		
Process owners	■	■	■	■	■	■	■	■	■	■
Quality consultants	■	■	■	■	■	■	■	■	■	■
Senior management	■	■			■	■	■	■		■
Sponsor	■	■	■	■	■	■	■	■	■	■
Stakeholders			■		■	■	■	■		
Operational planners	■	■					■	■		
Implementation team								■	■	■

Benchmarking: Supporting a Total Quality Approach

Leave the beaten path occasionally and dive into the woods. You will be certain to find something you have never seen before.

Alexander Graham Bell

Bell's "walks in the woods" were the first steps for a business built on discovery and innovation. As divestiture, redirection, and globalization have made change a constant force in our business, our founder's century-old invitation to leave the beaten path takes on a new urgency and relevance.

AT&T has developed a Total Quality Approach to manage change as a positive force. Creative change, continuous change, change directed by quality principles and practices, is our strategy for continuous improvement of our processes and our business. Benchmarking—looking beyond the beaten track— is a key element of business planning and process management models that support creative change. The AT&T Benchmarking Process enables our business leaders and process teams to make effective use of a world of ideas and insights to plan and manage change for continuous improvement.

Part I introduces the benchmarking process as an integral activity in a Total Quality Approach to doing business.

Introduction to Benchmarking

What is bench–marking?

Benchmarking is a process for continuously measuring a company's current business operations and comparing them to best-in-class operations. The insights gained from benchmarking provide organizations with a foundation for building operational plans to meet and surpass industry best practices. The most important aspects of any benchmarking process include planning, collecting benchmarking information, using benchmarking information, and updating the information.

Why benchmark?

United States companies increasingly integrate benchmarking with their business planning processes in response to:

- The competitive nature of global business.

- Heightened understanding that competitive advantage requires aggressive improvement of practices to world-class standards.

The Malcolm Baldrige National Quality Award (MBNQA) criteria are widely endorsed as a test of a business' ability to meet world-class standards. These criteria identify benchmarking as a fundamental and necessary process in support of business and quality management.

> *Benchmarks offer the opportunity to achieve significant improvements based on adoption or adaptation of current best practice...benchmarks represent a clear challenge to "beat the best," thus encouraging major improvements rather than only incremental refinements of existing approaches.* [1]

Over 25 percent of the total MBNQA point score is based on how effectively the business collects and uses benchmark data.

Within AT&T, the Chairman's Quality Award, based on the MBNQA criteria, evaluates benchmarking activities as part of an overall assessment of individual business unit quality management practices.

Benchmarking for Business Planning

Overview

In addition to stimulating learning, innovation, and change, benchmarking provides insights and data for direction setting, process management, and process improvement. It supports every level of business planning: strategic, key process management, and operational. Benchmarking results are input to the planning process, and resulting plans suggest new directions for benchmarking activities.

Strategic planning

At the strategic level, a business sets its course. MBNQA categories that address leadership, strategic quality planning, human resource development and management, and customer focus and satisfaction provide a framework for assessing management processes at the strategic level.

A business assesses competitors, customer needs, environment, technology, industry, economy, and shareholder interests to set its vision, mission, goals, objectives, and guiding principles. The business also uses this information to establish customer requirements, shareholder requirements, competitive positioning, pricing, key performance indicators, core competencies, and its overall quality and management system.

Benchmarking supports the strategic level of a business by complementing the assessment phase of the business planning process. For example, findings from benchmarking enable a company to set realistic targets for corporate performance over a three- to five-year period, determine the appropriate product/service mix, or close the gap between competitors and the company's own business.

Key process management planning

Key business processes are cross-functional processes critical to satisfying customers, maintaining competitive effectiveness, or achieving strategic goals. Examples include order fulfillment, customer service, and new product introduction. (*Leading the Quality Initiative*[2] offers an in-depth discussion of key business processes.) MBNQA categories that address information and analysis, management of process quality, quality and operational results, and customer focus and satisfaction provide a framework for assessing key business processes.

Key process management focuses on the horizontal activity in an organization or business, the flow of ideas, information, and products across the various development, purchasing, manufacturing, sales, and services organizations. To deliver a quality product or service, the company must have an integrated approach to managing quality across all associated processes and operations.[3]

At the key process management level, benchmarking promotes sharing across diverse organizations within a company. When several organizations form a team to benchmark a key process issue, each related organization benefits from the project's results. Partnerships among organizations with similar key processes eliminate the costs to the company for duplication of effort.

Operational planning

Planning at the operational level addresses the business' day-to-day activities. MBNQA categories that evaluate information and analysis, management of process quality, quality and operational results, and customer focus and satisfaction provide a framework for assessing processes at this planning level. Examples of operational level processes include customer complaint handling, software change management, and employee expense tracking.

Benchmarking supports the operational level by providing process management teams with a view of how other organizations (internal and external) perform similar operations. Findings may enable breakthrough improvements in day-to-day operations.

Impact to the organization

Benchmarking helps a business to learn and change in different ways. Depending on the level of business planning at which it is applied, it supports one of four types of organizational change:[4]

- Reorientation, based on strategic/breakthrough thinking in anticipation of change (for example, expansion into new markets by capitalizing on a best-in-class process).

- Re-creation, based on strategic/breakthrough thinking in reaction to market or environmental change (for example, the Xerox copier business' dramatic recovery in the 1980s).

- Tuning, based on incremental improvements in anticipation of change (for example, companies recognized for best-in-class processes continue to perform benchmarking).

- Adaptation, based on incremental improvements in reaction to market or environmental change (for example, benchmarking to ensure continuing compliance with environmental policies).

Benchmarking performed at the strategic level leads to reorientation and re-creation. At the operational level, expect change in the form of tuning and adapting business processes.

Is Your Business Ready to Benchmark?

Value to the business

There is always value in gaining a new perspective, measuring ourselves against the best, and discovering ideas and practices that can help us to improve. A business will reap the fullest benefits from a benchmarking process, however, within the framework of a sound, well-deployed quality system.

Assessing your business

The AT&T Quality Evolution Model is an effective tool for assessing your business' readiness to undertake benchmarking. As described in the AT&T *Quality Manager's Handbook*,[5] a business quality management system matures predictably through four phases:

Awareness: Characteristics of a business in the Awareness phase include indirect or inadequate communication, limited implementation of process and quality management, and no consistent approach to customer and supplier relationships.

The Baldrige score in this phase is well below 400 points.

Knowledge: In the Knowledge phase, the business understands customers, suppliers, and processes, and business activities focus on customer requirements.

Baldrige scores range from 400 to 600 points.

Wisdom: Cooperation, empowerment, and partnership with customers and suppliers for mutual advantage characterize the business that has advanced to the Wisdom phase.

Baldrige scores reach 600 to 800 points.

World-Class: A passionate dedication to maintaining world-class status, true teamwork with customers and suppliers, and customer-driven goals and objectives are hallmarks of the world-class business.

Baldrige scores are 800 points and better.

Benefits in each phase

This book describes a process that integrates the search for best practices in a systematic approach that leads to:

- A deeper understanding of customers, processes, and measures that will focus benchmarking efforts on identifying dramatic improvement opportunities and breakthroughs at key process and strategic levels.

- Systems and capabilities that will enable them to use benchmarking results effectively at key process and strategic levels.

Phase	Benchmarking Activities
Awareness	Are typically single-execution events such as literature searches or executive visits; can be of value in specific processes or operations, where manager or team is positioned to implement findings; substantial improvements at strategic and key process levels require senior management involvement.
Knowledge	Can achieve breakthrough improvements in stable processes and operations; existing process measures facilitate comparison and evaluation of benchmarking results. Senior management involvement may be required at key process and strategic levels.
Wisdom	Are integrated with continuous improvement approach to managing processes and operations; substantial improvements and breakthroughs possible at key process level.
World-Class	Are integrated with business planning process; well-focused, with constant improvement of practices and broad participation throughout business in forums, associations, and activities that yield information about new practices.

The AT&T Benchmarking Process

Overview

The AT&T benchmarking process complements AT&T process management and quality system models. The benchmarking process:

- Builds on process and business planning information to identify directions for the benchmarking activity.

- Develops information that serves as input to further planning and improvement.

This section introduces the benchmarking process model and activities and establishes the relationship between benchmarking and process management. Part II of this book provides detailed information on each step in the benchmarking process.

Process model

This illustration represents the benchmarking process as a cycle, a perspective that encourages the continuous evaluation required to recognize additional opportunities for improvement.

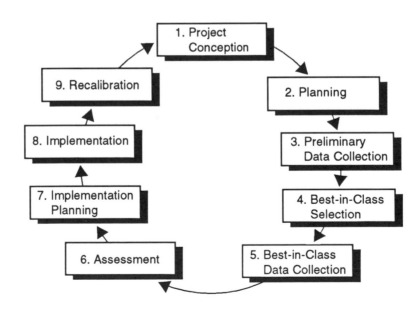

Process overview

This table summarizes activities in each step of the benchmarking process.

Step		Activity
1	Project Conception	Identify need and decide to benchmark.
2	Planning	Determine scope, objectives and develop a benchmarking plan.
3	Preliminary Data Collection	Collect data on industry, companies, and similar internal processes; collect detailed data on own process.
4	Best-in-Class Selection	Select companies with best-in-class processes.
5	Best-in-Class Data Collection	Collect detailed data from companies with best-in-class processes.
6	Assessment	Compare own and best-in-class processes; develop recommendations.
7	Implementation Planning	Develop operational improvement plans to attain superior performance.
8	Implementation	Enact operational plans and monitor process improvements.
9	Recalibration	Update benchmarking findings and assess improved process.

Benchmarking and process management

The benchmarking process extends beyond identifying targets and goals to a systematic approach for collecting, applying, and maintaining benchmarking data. Within the context of process management, the benchmarking process yields not just anecdotal information, but focused and immediately useful results.

Benchmarking is not an alternative to process management; rather it provides the external focus that helps to identify improvement opportunities. Using AT&T's process management methodology (PQMI)[6] as a frame of reference, benchmarking is especially critical between Step 4 (Assess conformance to customer requirements) and Step 5 (Investigate process improvement opportunities). Organizations that have completed Steps 1 through 4 of PQMI may find some of the sub-activities in the planning steps of the benchmarking process unnecessary.

PQMI

1: Establish Process Management Responsibilities
2: Define Process and Identify Customer Requirements
3: Define and Establish Measures
4: Assess Conformance To Customer Requirements
5: Investigate Process Improvement Opportunities
6: Rank Improvement and Set Objectives
7: Improve Process Quality

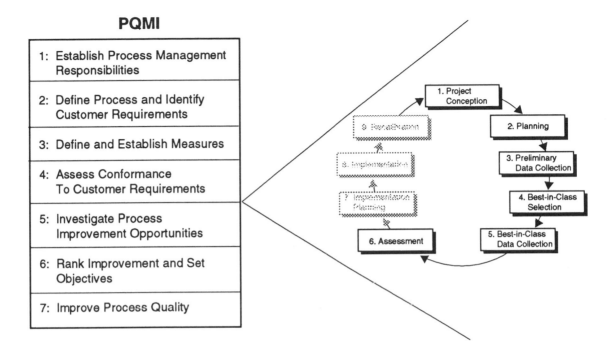

Merging the steps of PQMI with the external focus and insights of benchmarking offers great potential to adapt the best of the best and to achieve superior process performance. Organizations that are already skilled and involved in PQMI are well positioned to successfully execute the benchmarking process.

Steps 1 through 4 of PQMI establish process ownership and the process baseline. Process management teams at this stage have a solid understanding of customers, suppliers, major processes, and measurements. They have also collected and reviewed measurement data on process outputs.

This information is critical input to the initial steps of benchmarking, providing a baseline for evaluating current position relative to the competition and best-in-class organizations. Benchmarking encourages the study of practices that lead to best-in-class performance, so improvements or breakthroughs can be identified and incorporated into process and operational plans. When the benchmarking process is used within the context of PQMI, the benchmarking process ends with Step 6 (Assessment). Activities within steps 7 through 9 of the benchmarking process are addressed in the latter steps of PQMI.

Managing the Benchmarking Process

Project view
Benchmarking is a process for *continuously* measuring a company's current business operations and comparing them to best-in-class operations. However, as part of your business planning and process management planning processes, each cycle of benchmarking activity may be viewed and managed as a separate project (even if it is integrated into the ongoing work activities of an organization). Most of the following conditions apply to managing benchmarking projects:

- Each execution of the benchmarking process is a unique, one-time event incorporated into your planning process.

- Each execution has a specific start and end (Step 1 through Step 6 or Step 9).

- The scope of work can be categorized into definable tasks.

- A specific budget is allocated to conduct benchmarking.

- It often requires the use of multiple and shared resources.

- It may require the establishment of a benchmarking project team.[7]

When to benchmark
The planning process can include elements such as time, performance levels, and new opportunities that are monitored throughout the planning cycle to determine when benchmarking should be undertaken. For instance, in a volatile area such as new software development, benchmarking may be triggered by time (every year), by new practices (ongoing secondary research), and by customer satisfaction levels (fluctuating below target level).

Legal issues
Because benchmarking involves the exchange of potentially sensitive information, it must be governed by a set of basic legal principles, ethical standards, competitive guidelines, and intellectual property considerations that serve to:

- Safeguard the business from an inappropriate approach to a benchmarking partner, a particularly critical concern if the proposed benchmarking partner is a potential or direct competitor. This type of benchmarking requires compliance with strict legal and competitive guidelines; legal counsel should be sought whenever you are considering contacting competitors.

■ Protect your benchmarking partners' competitive information. You should avoid receiving proprietary information from another company, and you must fulfill all obligations and agreements about use of information. For example, your benchmark partner may ask you to refrain from sharing its information with other organizations in your company that it views as competitors.

Legal considerations are described in greater detail in the Appendix.

The Benchmarking Process

Continuous quality improvement is an ongoing journey of discovery, a cycle of developing quality plans, implementing and evaluating those plans, and improving them based on the results and changes in the business.

In the spirit of continuous improvement, the AT&T Benchmarking Process provides a systematic approach for gathering and applying data from sources outside the organization and integrating them with other internal quality improvement activities. This benchmarking cycle includes activities for planning and focusing a benchmarking activity, collecting data on world-class processes, comparing world-class data to existing processes, developing and implementing improvement plans, and updating the findings to identify additional improvement opportunities and set an interval for the next benchmarking activity.

Part II details the nine-step AT&T Benchmarking Process.

Project Conception

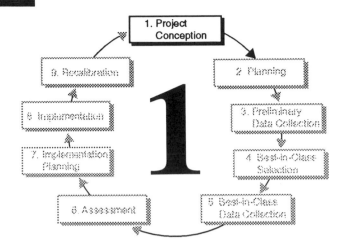

The challenge is to view every element of every operation through a customer's lens; to constantly attempt to—literally—redefine each element of the business in terms of the customer's perceptions of the intangibles.

Tom Peters
Thriving on Chaos

Activities in Step 1

Step 1 outlines the preliminary activities that help you:

- Understand the elements of successful benchmarking.
- Determine whether you are ready to benchmark.
- Determine the scope and urgency of the particular benchmarking activity you are planning.
- Obtain a preliminary commitment of planning resources.
- Identify all stakeholders and potential participants.
- Establish a general set of goals, objectives, and constraints.
- Plan a kick-off meeting.

Inputs

To begin the project conception step, you should understand:

- The organization's vision, mission, and goals.
- The catalyst that is driving the benchmarking activity.

Vision, mission, and goals

Benchmarking flows from business vision, mission, goals, strategies, and priorities. Use these to establish benchmarking objectives that meet the needs of your customers and business. An organization is not ready to benchmark if its vision, mission, and goals have not yet been established.

A catalyst

A catalyst increases the rate of a chemical reaction without being consumed by the process. In your organization, a catalyst is the impetus that "gets the ball rolling." Without it, the tension in the organization often is not elevated enough to encourage change.

Catalysts for benchmarking may include:

- A planning process that encourages an external focus.
- Changing or emerging customer needs.
- A shift in strategic direction.
- Mounting business problems.
- Newly recognized business opportunities.
- Dissatisfaction with current conditions.
- Impending business failure.
- An individual who is a champion of benchmarking.
- A recalibration plan (discussed in detail in Chapter 9).

Elements of Effective Benchmarking

Critical attributes

Does your organization have the proper environment for effective benchmarking? Can it be created?

Five attributes contribute to making your benchmarking effort more effective:

- Senior management commitment.
- Active involvement.
- Personal commitment.
- Adherence to a benchmarking process.
- Effective communication.

Committed senior management

The first step you should take in initiating a benchmarking activity is to obtain the commitment of senior management. Senior management must support benchmarking by committing time, allocating sufficient resources, removing obstacles, encouraging communication, and rewarding the effort. Senior management must recognize that, as a natural outflow of the business planning process, this may entail a shift in priorities and resources from other assignments.

Senior management can demonstrate this commitment by:

- Providing a sponsor.
- Selecting a benchmarking leader.
- Committing resources.
- Communicating successes.

Selecting the sponsor

A sponsor funds the project and assumes responsibility for the benchmarking effort and results. Senior management should try to select a sponsor with the influence to keep up the momentum. Sponsors are often the process owners who are responsible for managing the process being benchmarked and implementing improvement opportunities. They can make change happen because they have the position and power to do so.

Also solicit the support of a champion. A champion initially defends the benchmarking effort and later helps remove obstacles along the way. Champions are typically process or sub-process owners, process team leaders, subject matter experts, or managers in influential positions.

17

If a champion initiated the idea, then he or she may be in the best position to ensure that senior management maintains an ongoing commitment to benchmarking.

Selecting a benchmarking leader

The benchmarking leader is responsible for managing the benchmarking project. This leader should be either the owner of the process that is being benchmarked, or an assigned project manager who is supported by the sponsor and process owner. In instances where more than one process is affected, process owners may share the role of leading the benchmarking team. The leader must be in a position to implement change in all areas that will be examined and affected. This is particularly important if more than one organization or process is involved.

Committing resources

Tentative resources such as time, money, people, and systems should be assigned during Step 1 and then refined and committed to during the planning step (see Chapter 2). Resource commitment depends on several factors, including the planned extent of the benchmarking activity, the number of people that will be involved, and previous benchmarking experience. Establish the priority of this project relative to other parallel activities occurring within the organization.

Communicating successes

Because benchmarking is a continuous learning process, it is important to start small and set milestones. Senior management should encourage the sponsor and team to communicate even small successes to the organization to sustain enthusiasm.

Active involvement

Approach the benchmarking process in a manner that encourages the active involvement of:

- Customers for defining and clarifying needs.
- Senior management for setting direction.
- Process owners for defining current processes, goals, and performance.
- All others who have a stake in the results.

The active involvement of those who may be affected by the benchmarking findings wins acceptance for the findings and the implementation of improvement opportunities.

Personal commitment

New and innovative ideas generated during the benchmarking process may lead to significant change. While many find the learning process exciting, some people may become nervous and defensive at the prospect of change. To encourage a receptive environment, it is important for the team and those affected by the activity to make a personal commitment to learn, change, remain open-minded, take some risk, and be patient. Keep in mind that benchmarking can reduce the risk involved with change because it involves a systematic process that captures practices that have been proven to work effectively in other places.

Benchmarking process

Before initiating a benchmarking activity, all participants should agree on the approach. The process described in this book serves as a systematic framework that can be customized to your particular activity. Careful planning helps avoid confusion about what activities should take place, who should perform them, and how to act on the findings.

Effective communication

Throughout the benchmarking activity, the sponsor and team should continuously and effectively communicate with their stakeholders. This leads stakeholders to accept benchmarking findings and recommendations, identify improvement opportunities, develop operational plans, and successfully implement changes.

Deciding to Benchmark

Setting goals

Once senior management decides the organization can benefit from benchmarking and has created the proper environment, it is important to develop a general set of goals for the benchmarking activity. These goals must be consistent with the organization's business objectives.

Determining the scope

Deciding what to benchmark *must* precede the identification of companies to benchmark. Potential processes, functions, products, or services to benchmark should be evaluated and ranked based on relevancy, importance, and validity with respect to the organization's business objectives. A process management methodology (such as PQMI Steps 1 through 4) helps management identify appropriate benchmarking projects.

In trying to identify the benchmarking project scope, consider the following questions:

- Is it likely that this benchmarking project will measurably improve customer satisfaction for a given function, process, product, or service?

- Is it likely that this benchmarking project will measurably improve the organization's ability to achieve its goals? In the short-term? In the longer-term?

- Is it likely that this benchmarking project will significantly influence current business plans and actions?

If your benchmarking project is large and complex, consider reducing the scope further. Subsequent benchmarking projects can be formed to address additional key focus areas.

Estimating resource requirements

Like all work processes, resource requirements depend on several variables. Obviously, the more complex the benchmarking process is, the more time, money, and people are required to complete the activity properly.

To estimate resource requirements, consider the following factors:

Some Factors That Decrease the Required Resources	Some Factors That Increase the Required Resources
■ A quality approach is effectively in place	■ No common quality approach exists
■ The scope is limited	■ The scope is not well-defined
■ Few organizations or processes are affected	■ A key process or cross-functional process is affected
■ Few people are involved	■ Many people are involved and affected
■ Only telephone interviews and research will be conducted	■ Visit coordination and scheduling is expected
■ The team has experience in benchmarking	■ Benchmarking is new to the organization
■ The team is dedicated solely to this project	■ The team is not dedicated solely to the project

Setting the schedule

A benchmarking project that includes visits to external companies, a limited scope, and a dedicated, full-time team may take 12 to 24 weeks. You can reduce that time frame to 8 to 15 weeks if all the factors that decrease required resources listed above are in place.

A program coordinator assigned full-time typically requires anywhere from 6 to 18 months to establish an ongoing program of coordinated benchmarking projects within an organization.

Involving the Right People

Makeup of the team

The scope of your effort, available resources, and overall objectives determine the appropriate composition for your benchmarking team. You may have:

- An individual who is responsible for conducting the benchmarking project and presenting the findings to the sponsor or process owner.

- An external consultant who is responsible for conducting the benchmarking project and presenting the findings to the sponsor or process owner.

- A benchmarking team that is responsible for conducting the benchmarking project and presenting the findings to the sponsor or process owner.

- A process team that is responsible for process management and conducting the benchmarking project before proceeding to selection of improvement opportunities.

- A benchmarking team and stakeholder team that are responsible for conducting the benchmarking project, presenting the findings, and implementing operational plans.

- A core team and set of benchmarking teams that are responsible for organizing and coordinating a series of benchmarking projects, identifying improvement opportunities, and implementing operational plans.

Factors to consider

Each option presents its own set of advantages and disadvantages.

Options	Advantages	Disadvantages
Individual	■ Not as dependent on other people ■ Helps focus project ■ Less outside interference ■ Easier to plan, schedule, & make decisions	■ Minimizes stakeholder involvement ■ May become derailed ■ Limited viewpoint ■ Difficult to implement plans
External Consultant	■ May be fast ■ Helps focus project ■ No outside interference ■ Easier to plan, schedule, & make decisions	■ Minimizes involvement ■ May become derailed ■ Usually expensive ■ May not understand internal processes ■ May not understand consultant's findings ■ Difficult to implement plans
Benchmarking Team	■ Fast ■ Active involvement ■ Greater innovation ■ Limited outside interference ■ Easier to plan & schedule, ■ Natural alignment with sponsors	■ More resources ■ Some start-up time ■ Harder to make decisions ■ Roles & responsibilities may be unclear
Process Team	■ Fast ■ Active involvement ■ Greater innovation ■ Limited outside interference ■ Easier to plan, schedule, & make decisions ■ Natural alignment with process owner	■ May divert attention from quick incremental improvements ■ Process team takes time to do benchmarking versus setting up a project team
Benchmarking Team and Stakeholder Team	■ Active involvement ■ Easier to implement ■ Greater innovation	■ Takes more time ■ Harder to plan, schedule, & make decisions
Core Team & Set of Benchmarking Teams	■ Active involvement ■ If well-orchestrated, associated areas are addressed ■ Can tackle large problem areas ■ Maximum impact	■ Time impediments ■ Risky ■ Difficult to plan, schedule, & make decisions

Forming the Team

Include all stakeholders

Consider the different needs of all stakeholders involved in the activity and determine whether they should participate on the benchmarking team. As an alternative to active team participation, identify a method of communicating with those who must at least stay informed. Stakeholders can include customers, suppliers/partners, experts, and derailers.

Customers

Customers, in this instance, are those who commission the benchmarking activity, contribute requirements and feedback to your process, or are beneficiaries of the results. This may include the process owner if he or she is not leading the benchmarking project. You should:

- Involve them in defining the scope and success criteria.
- Communicate progress.
- Ask them to review intermediate work products.
- Reconfirm the success criteria with them periodically.
- Prepare them for results.

When possible, allow customers to choose whether they have active representation on the benchmarking team.

Suppliers/ partners

Suppliers and partners provide the tangible inputs and crucial services required to effectively complete the benchmarking activity. For example, library services can provide secondary research reports on the industry or prior benchmarking studies; process management teams can characterize, define, and provide a baseline for the process to be benchmarked. Suppliers and partners may also be customers of the output from the benchmarking activity.

Make suppliers and partners an integral part of planning even if they are not participants on the benchmarking team. Work with them to determine clear, explicit requirements for what is needed, when it is needed, and who is responsible for taking action. Understand their needs, and clearly communicate to them how they share credit for the activity's success.

Experts

Experts have valuable experience to offer to a benchmarking activity. They understand where process improvements may be needed and can help focus the effort. Their agreement may be required for acceptance of results. Like customers, you should:

- Involve them in planning the project and defining success criteria.

- Ask them to define the detailed questions to be answered by the benchmarking activity.

- Ask them to review intermediate work products.

- Reconfirm the success criteria with them periodically.

- Keep them informed on pending results.

This group may serve as a pool of "auxiliary members" that support data collection and assessment activities.

Derailers

Anyone who may be affected by the findings from benchmarking is a potential derailer. They may be non-believers; they may be concerned about the effect change has on their jobs or the size and structure of their organization; or they may believe that they already have enough information to make decisions.

Address their concerns early in the process. The Process Decision Program Chart (PDPC) Policy Deployment planning tool may be useful in identifying conceivable objections and contingencies in response to these objections.[8] Their direct participation in the project may help to increase their buy-in.

Roles and responsibilities

It is important for all benchmarking participants to understand their roles in the benchmarking activity. Use the following list as a starting point for assigning general responsibilities to each team member. Refer to *The AT&T QIT Helper*[9] for more suggestions about how to organize your team.

Player	Responsibility
Sponsor (often is the process owner or the process owner's manager)	■ Funds the benchmarking activity and accounts for results ■ Uses power to make change happen ■ Communicates with and supports team leader ■ Ensures management commitment to benchmarking ■ Reviews progress and communicates it to the larger organization ■ Reviews benchmarking findings
Champion (often initiates a benchmarking effort)	■ Defends benchmarking effort ■ Removes obstacles along the way ■ Communicates with and supports team leader
Team Leader (may be the process owner)	■ Communicates with sponsor ■ Leads and facilitates the team ■ Ensures active stakeholder involvement ■ Ensures active team involvement ■ Negotiates with sponsor, management, and team ■ Oversees administration of team logistics, meetings, and progress reports
Team Member	■ Shares knowledge and expertise ■ Asks questions and probes for answers ■ Makes a personal commitment ■ Encourages a mutual exchange of ideas ■ Respects the dignity of other members ■ Conveys information to and from home organization
Consultant (internal or external)	■ Shares knowledge and expertise on benchmarking process ■ Coaches, facilitates, and instructs team ■ Supports the leader ■ May set up company visits

Kick-off meeting

The first meeting of the team is a great opportunity to bring the sponsor, champion, advocates, and team together to generate enthusiasm and set the stage for successful benchmarking. Provide an overview of the benchmarking process for team members who have not had prior benchmarking training or experience. It ensures that the team shares a common understanding of the process. If possible, continue to meet in the same room, keep results visible, and keep the team anchored in the process.

Checkpoint

Before you begin the next step, the initiator of the benchmarking activity should:

- Negotiate and allocate planning resources with the sponsor.

- Obtain stakeholder support.

Planning

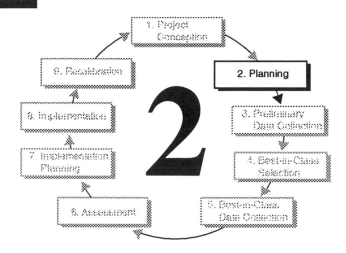

Pick battles big enough to matter, small enough to win.

Jonathan Kozol
Illiterate America

Activities in Step 2

In Step 2, the benchmarking team further defines the scope and develops the benchmarking project plan. The team should present the full plan to stakeholders to obtain their support and commitment.

Step 2 outlines the activities that help the benchmarking team:

- Obtain commitment from stakeholders.
- Stabilize the benchmarking team list.
- Formulate the project plan.

Inputs

To begin the planning step, the benchmarking team should have:

- An understanding of why and how the benchmarking project was conceived and the problem being addressed.

- Identified the owner, sponsor and/or champion, and benchmarking leader.

- A confirmed list of benchmarking team members.

- A general set of goals and objectives for the project.

- An indication of the scope and urgency of the benchmarking activity and resources available.

- Customer requirements (output of PQMI Step 2: define process and identify customer requirements).

- Process definition (output of PQMI Step 2).

- Held a kick-off meeting.

- Provided benchmarking training for team members (see Appendix).

Developing the Project Plan

Elements of the project plan

The project plan should articulate:

- Goals and objectives.
- Scope and resources.
- Key players.
- Critical success factors.
- Core competencies.
- Roles and responsibilities.
- Improvement opportunities.
- Milestones and deliverables.
- Performance measures.
- Communication activities.
- Contingency plans.

The benchmarking project plan is similar to project plans for process improvement activities. A template to aid in creating this plan appears in the Appendix.

Setting goals and objectives

Considering the scope of the project, set goals and target objectives for the overall benchmarking process and each step. Be sure that these are measurable and realistic. For example, establish a target date for collecting all data (Step 5, completion) that allows enough time for secondary research, visit preparation, scheduling, and visits. These may need to be adjusted later.

Refining the scope

Refine the scope to focus on a manageable set of benchmarking areas of strong importance to the organization. It is necessary to narrow the scope to a few key areas of the process because benchmarking all aspects of an organization's operation would generally be extremely difficult and prohibitive in cost.

Consider the critical success factors based on customer requirements, core competencies, and key improvement opportunities.

Confirming resources

Once the team members refine the scope and understand the needs for the benchmarking activity, they may need to renegotiate for additional resources. This information should appear in the plan.

Listing key players

In the project plan, provide names of the owner, sponsor, customers, and benchmarking team members identified in Chapter 1. Select additional team members whose backgrounds closely match the scope of investigation and auxiliary members whose expertise may be needed during periods of the benchmarking activity. Also, outline any concerns over ownership or sponsorship before proceeding.

Critical success factors

Critical success factors are the few key areas that are required for the organization's success. Although these may have been addressed in the organization's strategic or business plan, they bear revisiting at the start of the benchmarking activity. The critical success factor concept assumes that the Pareto Principle is in effect. The Pareto Principle, which Juran also refers to as the principle of the "vital few," holds that a few critical factors are largely responsible for the results. The Pareto diagram is frequently used as a tool for identifying the critical factors that have the greatest impact.[10] The organization's business plans and customer surveys are excellent sources to guide the team's determination of those areas critical to the success of the organization.

Examples of critical success factors may be:

- *Superior customer relations*—of general importance, critical in high technology areas requiring extensive customer support and custom product areas like systems integration.

- *Productivity, efficiency*—important in highly competitive manufacturing businesses like consumer electronics and in large-scale systems development.

- *New products and shortened cycle times*—important in highly competitive technology-based businesses like consumer electronics and autos, also in custom product areas like systems integration.

- *Technological capabilities*—important in high-tech businesses (supercomputers, large-scale software, and consumer electronics).

Core competencies	Core competencies are the collective learning in the organization. Core competencies provide potential access to a wide variety of markets, make a significant contribution to value as perceived by the customer, and should be difficult for competitors to imitate.[11]

Examples of core competencies include:

- The ability to develop and deliver new and high performance technologies.

- The ability to manufacture highly reliable products.

- An efficient distribution network.

- Exceptional customer service.

Improvement opportunities	If improvement opportunities have not been identified, they can be identified through standard process management activities and ranked using techniques such as brainstorming, force-field analysis, and multivoting quality tools.

Examples of improvement opportunities include:

- More efficient communication between customer service and technical representatives.

- More effective requests for proposals.

- A more effective quality management and improvement process.

- Enhanced sales presentations.

- Greater recognition of employees.

The critical success factors, core competencies, and improvement opportunities are used to rank areas of focus. The following are areas of focus that might be identified by this process:

- *Improve a core competency or strength for additional payoff*—for example, increased ability to generate custom features.

- *Improvement opportunity that could be detrimental to long-term success if left unaddressed*—for example, high cost in a market that is expected to become price competitive.

- *Future critical success factor*—for example, ability to successfully manage global human resources in an increasingly global competitive environment.

- *Critical success factor that is not currently addressed*—for example, highly responsive customer support services.

Defining roles and responsi–bilities

The plan must clearly define and articulate agreed-upon roles and responsibilities of all players and stakeholders, including specific deliverables and resource commitments. If the process owner is not on the benchmarking team, the communication process and responsibility for communicating with the process owner must be clearly defined.

Benchmarking data provides status relative to best-in-class processes, which must then be driven to operational plans. Using benchmarking findings and recommendations to revise existing processes is the responsibility of senior management, the sponsor, and process owner, and should be agreed to in the planning stage.

Identifying deliverables

Identify deliverables that typically include:

- A project plan.

- Detailed process diagrams and flowcharts for your own business process.

- Performance metrics (baseline data).

- Secondary research.

- Best-in-class selection criteria and matrix.

- Best-in-class selections.

- Topic areas and question sets.

- Briefing packages.

- Visit reports.

- Assessment report (including gap analysis).

- Recommendations.

- Operational plans that describe the new process.

- Implementation plans to set the operational plans in place.

- Progress reports.
- A recalibration plan.

The remaining chapters of this book describe each of these deliverables in detail.

Establishing performance measurements

Include a preliminary list of measures that helps you compare the performance of your process to that of best-in-class processes. Consider measures that address both efficiency and effectiveness of the process.

Measures of efficiency often track human resources. For example, an efficiency measure for an order-taking process might be the number of calls answered hourly per agent. Select measures that clearly relate to stated business and benchmarking objectives.

Measures of effectiveness often address customer deliverables. For example, an effectiveness measure for a payroll system, based on customer requirements, might include the capability for electronic funds transfer to more than one financial institution. Another effectiveness measure is evaluating if customers are satisfied with the telephone manner of telemarketing representatives.

Examples of performance metrics are:

- Earnings to revenues.
- System response time.
- Dollars per transaction.
- Orders per hour.
- Number of features.
- Types of features.
- Number of sales leads.
- Project complexity.

Continuous communication

How can the team ensure that the benchmarking study does not become yet-another-report that contains findings that never get implemented? The sponsor and team members should communicate with stakeholders throughout the project to substantially improve the likelihood of successful implementation of benchmarking findings and recommendations. Key communication activities are listed on the next page.

- Assign responsibility for stakeholders who are not on the team to team members, the sponsor, the process owner, and the team leader as appropriate. Those assigned should be encouraged to:

  — Inform stakeholders of benchmarking developments at agreed upon milestones throughout the process.

  — Have continuous dialogue with stakeholders.

  — Ensure that stakeholders have enough time to contribute to and accept the approach.

  — Position the findings so that they are understood.

  — Ensure that recommendation and implementation plans are supported by stakeholders.

- Define interim deliverables to communicate progress to the entire stakeholder community.

- Develop and communicate an operational plan to continually improve to best-in-class. Set interim goals to close the gap and longer term goals to surpass competitors to become world class.

Contingency plans

During the planning phase, benchmarking teams should expect potential obstacles and develop contingency plans to address them. Consider contingencies for the following obstacles:

- Teams have an incomplete understanding of the benchmarking or business process.

- The organization has difficulty in focusing enough to effectively execute the benchmarking activity.

- The benchmarking activity may not be important enough to the business.

- Metrics may be too numerous to analyze, or poor in providing effective or useful comparisons. For example, software productivity measures may not include and account for substantial differences in overtime and maintenance activity.

- Stakeholders may not have enough involvement for the team to solicit their insights and secure buy-in.

- Customers' views may not have been considered in establishing the scope and evaluating performance. For example, the benchmarking team focuses on added feature diversity when customers may already find products complex and difficult to use.

Checkpoint   Before starting the next step, the initiator of the benchmarking activity should:

- Review the full project plan with management, stakeholders, and the team.
- Ensure senior management ownership and commitment through frequent communication and progress reports.
- Obtain stakeholder and team support.

Preliminary Data Collection

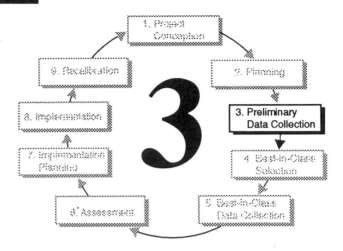

Creative solutions come more easily to minds prepared with knowledge.

Betty Edwards
Drawing on the Artist Within

Activities in Step 3

The team is prepared to gather data on industry performance and practices used within similar processes both internal and external to the business. During this step, the team also collects detailed data on its own business process. This preliminary data collection prepares the team for identifying best-in-class processes (Step 4) and for more detailed benchmarking information-gathering activities (Step 5).

Step 3 presents the activities that help the benchmarking team:

- Describe the current process.
- Develop selection criteria, topic areas, and question sets.
- Understand the types of data to collect.
- Collect secondary research data.

Inputs   To begin the preliminary data collection step, the team should have an
             agreed upon project plan.

Baselining Your Process

Why baseline?

To collect appropriate and useful data, the benchmarking team must understand the objectives and characteristics of the current process. The process baseline aids understanding and reduces the risk of poor subject and metric choices. *Note*: A process baseline may have already been created that the benchmarking team can use.

The baseline should identify:

- The objectives, customers, and requirements for the process.
- The workflow activities and responsibilities that comprise the process.
- The current measures and levels of performance.

Baseline elements

The baseline is crucial to the benchmarking activity because it provides the critical data that is used to begin the benchmarking process.

The baseline should identify:

- The objectives, customers, and requirements for the process.
- The workflow activities and responsibilities that comprise the process.
- The current measures and levels of performance.

Developing Selection Criteria

Description   Selection criteria are the set of definitive and limiting characteristics or performance metrics that help to screen and select processes that are worth further investigation. The criteria enable the benchmarking team to select processes that have successful achievements in the area being studied and aspects of their processes that can be directly compared to your process (analogs). Some examples of selection criteria are speed of delivery, global reputation, customer satisfaction, low number of software faults, and ability to attract and retain talented people.

During the development of the selection criteria, it is critical to involve the sponsor and key stakeholders so that there is common understanding of the rationale used to identify and select best-in-class processes. If these selection criteria are not tested with stakeholders, there may be later disagreement about the recommendations for best-in-class.

Selection criteria often include:

- Characteristics of your process, inputs, and outputs.
- Critical customer requirements.
- Characteristics of your critical success factors, core competencies, or improvement opportunities.
- Characteristics of your particular set of customers or suppliers.
- Process performance indicators or specific levels of performance.
- Environmental or cultural conditions.

Selecting and ranking criteria   Be sure to clearly define the criteria and their relative priority. Also, list a basic set of selection criteria that all companies must meet and a complementary set that only one or two companies might meet. This makes the final selection process easier. As you learn more from your research and data collection, you may want to add criteria. Limit your total selection criteria to between six and eight. Otherwise, the list becomes unmanageable and harder to assign priorities.

Example

Below is a sample set of selection criteria with definitions. The definitions are not strict, but they illustrate how the benchmarking team can adapt particular terms for its activity.

The focus of this example is to identify organizations with high quality and speed in software development.

Criteria	Team's Definition
Profitability*	Excellent, sound financial performance and sustained growth (expense-to-revenue ratio)
Cycle time	Recognized ability to turn around software in a timely fashion whether internally or in the marketplace
Defects to zero	Recognized ability to drive defects to zero
Information systems effectiveness	Ratings from various business magazines
Industry type	Predominant goods and services sold by company
Design team size	Average size of systems development team

* Note: Profitability information is based on public information such as annual reports and 10-K reports.

Selection matrix

One way to track the information during this discovery process, and facilitate the screening of that information later, is to begin developing a selection matrix for best-in-class. This matrix includes the list of criteria on one axis and a list of companies on the other as indicated in the sample matrix. A completed sample is shown in Chapter 4.

Sample best-in-class matrix

Criteria	Company A	Company B	Company C	Company D
Profitability				
Cycle time				
Defects to zero (per 1000 lines of code)				
Effectiveness				
Industry type				
Design team size				

Identifying Topic Areas

Creating a framework	A set of topic areas helps to focus the benchmarking team on in its benchmarking efforts. These topic areas can be viewed as an outline for organizing the data that will be collected based on the project objectives. Be sure to develop topics that address the elements defined in the scope, as well as uncommon issues or chronic problems in the current process. The topics should be defined so that they collectively span the set of information required to achieve benchmarking objectives.

Possible topics	Typical topic areas include:

- Corporate culture.

- Reward and recognition programs.

- Training.

- Cycle time.

- Measurement systems.

- Ownership and accountability.

According to the level of detail needed, limit topic areas to about five to ten. You may choose to refine these further as you pursue your data collection. Later, these serve as the basis of your initial discussions and letters to your potential benchmarking partners.

Preliminary question set	During the data collection process, develop a preliminary set of questions aligned with your topics. These will serve as a focus for the data you collect on internal and external processes in Step 5 (see Chapter 5).

The question set should be adapted to suit the type of data collection methodology you decide to use. For instance, a written survey may be structured differently from an interview guide used for in-person meetings. Sometimes a combination of methods works best. For example, a survey may be used to collect cost data and an interview guide may be used to collect process data.

As you collect data, you may find it necessary to revise your question set. This is a natural result of the learning you experience as you explore the variety of information sources available to you.

Types of Data to be Collected

Description During the preliminary data collection step, you should collect data on:

- Your own process.

- Analogous internal processes.

- Analogous processes in companies or organizations in your industry.

- Analogous processes in companies or organizations in other industries.

Your own process The importance of collecting data on your own process cannot be emphasized enough, particularly if you plan to talk to another company. Gathering information on your own process provides a rational basis for comparing it to the data you obtain from benchmarking. Without it, you cannot easily develop a convincing set of recommendations, action plans, and potential benefits. In addition, you need to be well-prepared to share information about your process to the same level of detail that you are requesting from others.

Analogous internal processes Analogous processes within the corporation are useful to consider, for the following reasons:

- Internal information exchanges are easier to arrange and allow more open sharing.

- Internal organizations provide a more risk-free forum for a trial run for your benchmarking team.

- Because internal organizations are likely to face similar objectives, environments, and constraints, lessons learned from internal benchmarks may have a greater likelihood of being directly implemented.

Industry Industry data includes information on similar processes from both your own specific industry, such as telecommunications and, more generally, in any business involved in process activities that are similar to your own. Organizations from other industries are more likely to provide a non-competitive and productive information exchange.

Industry data takes many forms, such as process innovations, trends, standards, and documented practices. In mature, established industries, process innovations often are found outside your own industry. Sources of information include professional associations and publications; government funded research and studies; business magazines; and federal, state, and local agencies. Additional sources include national, regional, and local newspapers; trade press; consultants; industry associates; customers; suppliers; and business partners.

Examples of industry data sources for large corporations and their standings are:

- "The Forbes 500" issued by *Forbes* magazine.

- "The Business Week Top 1000" issued by *Business Week* magazine.

- "The Fortune 500" issued by *Fortune* magazine.

- "Computerworld: The Premier 100" issued by *Computerworld* magazine.

Analogous processes in other organizations

As you probe for industry data, track the companies outside of your industry that are frequently cited in the literature or in discussions with subject matter experts. This helps you begin a list of target companies, divisions, or subgroups within a company that may have best-in-class processes and performance.

Keep in mind that these are not necessarily companies with best-in-class processes. Be aware of your information sources and their biases, and determine if information is valid. Look at a cross-section of sources to validate information. If your sources are varied, and the company's process is often cited, it becomes more likely you have discovered a best-in-class process.

In addition, you may already be aware of companies that have excellent reputations for the process you are benchmarking. Add these to your list and verify your research findings.

Note that you are building clues to determine which processes are best-in-class. Once you have limited your set of companies, further secondary research or subsequent primary research helps confirm which ones are best-in-class.

Do not limit your search to any one type of company. Consider both competitors and analogous companies in your search. Competitors are most difficult to solicit as benchmarking partners, but easier to analyze and compare results. You must contact your company's legal department before you approach competitors.

Analogs are those processes that have similar characteristics to your own processes. For example, a company that bottles soft drinks might examine how milk that originates from a dairy farmer gets bottled. Although their businesses are different, Xerox benchmarked L. L. Bean for its warehousing operation because it was an industry leader in that process.[12]

An approach for selecting analogs

To select analogs:

- Recall your process baseline (inputs to the process, the process itself, outputs of the process, and process requirements).

- Determine the general characteristics of your process (such as speed of delivery, type of suppliers, freshness).

- Based on these characteristics, brainstorm for types of companies that might have analogous operations (remember to think out of the box!).

- Validate your selections with research.

Sources and Techniques for Data Collection

Background

There are a wealth of sources and techniques for data collection, and selecting the right approach is a somewhat iterative process.

Research is not a purely scientific discipline. It involves degrees of creativity and art. Often, best-in-class processes are not readily definable or quantifiable. (This may be a sign that companies with best-in-class processes have room for improvement.) Do not minimize the value that can be provided by the probing skills of a research specialist.

Using a research specialist

Working with you, specialists are more apt to find key points and identify patterns and trends from secondary sources. A variety of sources should be used for validating key findings. Moreover, a research specialist is familiar with language used internally in an organization and can translate it to the corresponding terminology used in external publications. For example, *product realization* is a term often used within AT&T. Externally, though, this may be translated to *time-to-market* or *cycle time* or *speed of delivery*. The research specialist may also be able to ask clarifying questions to ease the search process and focus on what the customer really wants. For instance, a request for *customer service* information may, indeed, be a request for *customer satisfaction* or *complaint handling* or *customer service training* or *customer types*.

Establish a partnership with a research specialist at the start of your secondary research. By partnering, you capitalize on the specialist's expertise to achieve better coverage of your topic.

Typically, research specialists can obtain information such as employee numbers, and financial data from annual reports or 10-K reports and other sources within 24 hours. Within a few days they can provide information on processes, interpretive literature searches, article overviews, rating and ranking lists, or company overviews.

A time-consuming search may be necessary if it requires the research specialist to draw conclusions, read and synthesize data, formulate opinions, or conduct primary research. Performance data such as salary levels, department structure, number of people, and satisfaction rates may not be readily available if it is proprietary information or if it is information a company is only willing to share on a one-to-one basis with a benchmarking partner.

Tips for improving research results

When working with a research specialist, consider the following tips for improving your secondary research:

- Be aware that the level of detail on the information you request may only be available through primary sources.

- Allow enough lead time for the research specialist to gather and assemble the information.

- Provide as much detail as possible on the topic being researched and define terms.

- Stay involved and communicate often. Remember that this is an interactive process.

- Do not expect much performance data from secondary sources.

- Read or scan articles; often you may find gems or patterns.

- Be open-minded to explore new areas.

Information sources

In your search, be sure to include:

- Books, magazines, and journals.

- Business, industry, professional, and trade associations.

- Potential company contacts.

- Company libraries and research centers.

- Company benchmarking databases.

- Universities and colleges.

- Information clearinghouses.

- Competitive analysis reports or studies.

- Consultants.

- Corporate annual reports.

- Corporate financial results and 10-K reports.

- Customer satisfaction and research studies.

- Government publications.

- Information services within the corporation.

- Marketing research studies.

- National, regional, and local newspapers.
- On-line databases.
- Other groups within the corporation.
- Patent filings.
- Research grants.
- Technical journals.
- Trade associations.

Checkpoint Before beginning the next step, the benchmarking team should:

- Validate preliminary selection criteria with stakeholders.
- Communicate preliminary topics and question sets to stakeholders.
- Review baseline view of own process with stakeholders.
- Contact the legal department if you plan to approach competitors.

Best-In-Class Selection

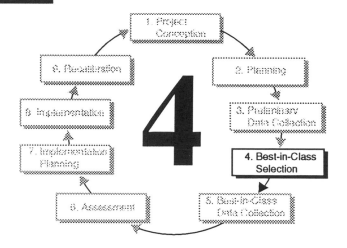

All the sources of innovative opportunity should be
systematically analyzed and systematically studied. It is not
enough to be alerted to them. The search has to be organized,
and must be done on a regular, systematic basis.

> Peter F. Drucker
> *Innovation and Entrepreneurship:*
> *Practice and Principles*

Activities in Step 4

Step 4 outlines the activities that help you:

- Select companies with best-in-class processes.
- Develop question sets for detailed data collection.

Inputs

To begin selecting companies with best-in-class processes, you should have:

- A current process description.
- A statement of scope (from your project plan).
- Preliminary selection criteria.
- Preliminary target companies with best-in-class processes.
- Preliminary topics and question sets.

Selecting Companies with Best-In-Class Processes

Description   The benchmarking team is now ready to screen for benchmarking opportunities and select a set of companies or organizations that have best-in-class processes based on research to date. The benchmarking team may have identified as few as 3 or as many as 25 companies (or divisions of large companies) to consider. Do not be overly concerned if there are only a few, especially if the area you are researching is new, limited, or unusual.

Refining the list   The team should now select three to six of the most promising companies' processes for further data collection. Often, this results in company visits. Several factors, such as time, complexity of the process being benchmarked, companies selected, and funding for travel, dictate how many processes should be examined and how many visits should take place.

Rank the list of companies based on the degree of fit to the selection criteria. If the benchmarking team defined a set of basic criteria that all companies must meet (see Chapter 3), then eliminate any company that does not meet that set of basic criteria.

Also, examine your selected set of companies' processes for breadth. For instance, consider companies that:

- Have processes with a proven track record of being best-in-class for a period of time.

- Have made substantial and successful process improvements.

- Represent a cross-section of industries.

- May not meet all the criteria, but have an innovative and apparently successful process.

Factors to consider   Consider the following additional factors to be sure the companies you select continue to meet your selection criteria further along in the process.

- *Is the company a Malcolm Baldrige National Quality Award winner?* Before scheduling a visit with these companies, check to see what internal and external information is available about them. Carefully examine data to see to what extent the Baldrige information supports your selection.

■ *Do your stakeholders view the company and its employees as credible and comparable?*
Again, to improve the likelihood that findings and recommendations are used, stakeholders must see that the information is relevant. If the stakeholders do not regard the selected company and its employees well, they will probably not value the resulting information.

■ *Is it in your company's business interest to support a benchmarking contact with the selected company at this time?*
Your sales account managers may be able to help you determine whether the company meets your selection criteria or who you may contact to negotiate an information exchange. More importantly, sales account managers may be aware of business issues that could constrain or be enhanced by potential benchmarking visits.

■ *Has anyone in your company recently visited the company you are benchmarking?*
If so, they may be able to provide a visit report. This information may be found through internal sources (databases, reports) and is useful if you still decide to visit. If the existing visit report contains answers to some of your original question set, you can focus on additional, more specific questions. You may also decide not to visit the company, particularly if the previous visit was recent and examined a similar process. Also, find out if relevant consultant reports exist.

Narrow your list of candidate companies to about six or eight companies. There is no guarantee that the companies you select have best-in-class processes, but a thorough research effort can increase the likelihood of a high-quality selection. Focus on your refined list for further research to validate that the processes are best-in-class.

Best-in-class selection matrix

Use the a sample of a completed best-in-class selection matrix below as a guideline for developing your own matrix. You may include weighted criteria and other data as well.

Criteria	Company A	Company B	Company C	Company D
Profitability	Excellent	Excellent	Excellent but Inconsistent	Excellent
Cycle Time	reduced 70-90% on average	improved throughput by 30%	average improvement 60% using CASE tools	6-7% improve–ment using new measurement system
Defects To Zero (Per 1000 Lines of Code)	.5	500 new programs with no failures		.2 - .4
Effectiveness	Top 10 in: ■ business magazine ■ computer magazine ■ consultant listing	Top 10 in: ■ business magazine ■ computer journal ■ consultant listing	Top 5 in: ■ business magazine ■ industry journal	Top 3 in: ■ business magazine ■ computer magazine
Industry Type	Banking	Pharmaceutical	Automotive	Electronics
Design Team Size		5-8 members		6-12 members

Before You Continue

Customizing the question set

In the previous step you developed a preliminary question set that serves as a foundation for building a customized question set for each company that you benchmark. The customized question sets may reflect:

- Additional probing based on new insights gained from further research.

- A core set of questions derived from the preliminary question set since some questions are not relevant for all companies.

- Additional questions particular to an individual benchmark company. For instance, if a company has specific process innovation they recently introduced, you may want to ask detailed questions about how they introduced the new process to their organization.

- Specific product names, service names, and terminology used within a company to demonstrate your knowledge about that company.

Legal review

Consider the importance of a review of your selected companies, customized question sets, and any material you plan to share with the appropriate legal and intellectual property representatives within your business. This is especially critical when planning a visit to a potential or direct competitor. When conducting competitive benchmarking, a company must ensure legal compliance and follow strict competitive, ethical, legal, and intellectual property guidelines. Refer to the the Appendix for more information on ethical and competitive guidelines.

Checkpoint

Before starting the next step, the benchmarking team should:

- Review with stakeholders the customized question sets and companies identified for data collection.

- Identify people in the company that are best suited to participate in specific visits.

- Contact your legal department if plans exist for approaching competitors and if question sets address sensitive information.

Best-in-Class Data Collection

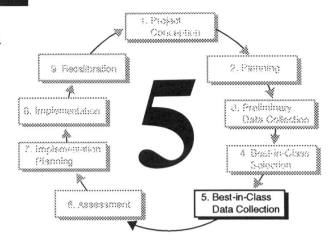

5. Best-in-Class
Data Collection

Benchmarking should be approached on a partnership basis in which both parties should expect to gain from the information sharing.

> Robert C. Camp
> *Benchmarking—the Search for Industry*
> *Best Practices that Lead to Superior Performance*

Activities in Step 5

Step 5 outlines the activities that help you:

- Understand approaches to detailed data collection.
- Plan and schedule company visits.
- Gather best-in-class process information from a visit.
- Prepare briefing packages and sessions.
- Manage effective interorganizational communication.

Inputs   To begin collecting best-in-class data, you should have:

- A list of selected companies with possible best-in-class processes.
- Customized question sets.

Collecting Detailed Data

Approaches for collecting data

The benchmarking team may elect one or several different approaches to collect detailed data about best-in-class processes. Generally, these include secondary data collection, questionnaires, telephone interviews, and company visits. Therefore, outputs are dependent upon the approach selected.

Your topic areas, question sets, and questionnaires provide the basis for collecting data on characteristics and performance levels for targeted companies.

Secondary data collection

You may find that review of existing reports and consultant interviews collected during your secondary research in Step 3 are sufficient for your data collection needs. This is certainly a consideration when your budget is limited and other data collection methods are cost prohibitive. These may also supplement the more detailed data collection approaches that follow.

For example, suppose you have selected four companies to visit for detailed data collection on their best-in-class processes. You discover that another unit in your company has already spoken to one of the four companies and has a visit report available. This gives you the latitude to use the information in your final report and to possibly choose another company on your list to visit.

Question-naires and telephone interviews

The use of mail questionnaires, telephone interviews, or focus groups may also be appropriate approaches to collecting detailed data on companies with best-in-class processes. If you choose any of these methods, your marketing research group is a useful resource to help you define, develop, design, test, conduct, and analyze your data collection using any of these methods. You may even choose to send a questionnaire to a company before a benchmarking visit. But, because these methods require proper design to be reliable, valid, and useful, you may have to solicit the help of a survey design consultant.

Company visits

Company visits (sometimes referred to as site visits) are usually the most useful means of collecting detailed data on companies. People become excited about what they hear, see things from a new perspective, have the opportunity to ask clarifying questions and take cues from body language. In addition, the company is often more candid in face-to-face discussions. Visits heighten the learning experience of those involved and help people

61

understand why changes in their own organization might be necessary and how these changes might be achieved.

Because company visits can influence the corporation's image with potential customers and provide information critical to the benchmarking activity, the visits require good planning and preparation. Refer to the Appendix for checklists and tips related to company visits.

Preparing for Company Visits

Elements of a successful visit

Planning, preparation, and the use of correct protocols create the proper environment for a successful visit and establish the rapport to support long-term partnerships needed to explore practices in depth. This section presents some simple guidelines, considerations, and suggestions that help your team develop a successful and professional approach to a company visit.

Schedule of company visits

It is likely that you will contact several companies and negotiate dates with several people. To simplify scheduling, use a scheduling tool (see Appendix for a sample) to:

- List all potential companies to be visited.

- Track company contacts (names, dates, status).

- Track tentative and confirmed visit dates.

- List tentative and confirmed attendees.

- Take special considerations into account (for example, limited time availability for a key participant).

Contacting companies

Your sales account managers can be extremely helpful in evaluating the business advisability of benchmarking within a specific company, and if favorable, in identifying the correct organization and person to contact. They may also test the company's environment for a potential visit. In some cases, they may even elect to make the initial contact for you.

Even if they are unable to provide a contact name, it is good practice to notify the appropriate sales account manager in your company *prior* to making initial contact. As a courtesy, keep the sales account manager informed of progress, meeting dates, attendees, and outcomes. The sales team should not participate in the benchmarking activity, even if the activity is remotely connected to sales, since it could hinder information sharing. In cases where the sales account manager has already established rapport with the individuals you are meeting with, both your group and the hosting group may elect to have the sales account manager attend.

Initial contact is usually made by telephone and is the responsibility of the benchmarking leader, team member, or consultant as determined in your benchmarking project plan. If the scope is broad and addresses multiple areas, the initial contact is often made by senior management or the unit

63

manager. If the scope is narrow or a relationship has already been established, you may choose to contact those individuals directly. They, in turn, should inform their management of the benchmarking activities.

Letters of request and confirmation

Following this conversation, send a letter to your contacts to confirm the understanding regarding your visit request. In this letter, include the objectives of the visit, the potential number of attendees, the background of organization and attendees, topic areas, and other relevant information. The letter may request specific participants from the other company, either directly or by function. Provide your partners with alternative dates that give them at least four weeks lead time to properly prepare for the meeting.

After an agreement is reached to conduct a company visit, send another letter to provide more detail about who is attending and the specific information your team would like to gather. This letter should contain enough information to enable your benchmarking partner to assemble the appropriate team of subject matter experts and to prepare for the session.

Propose a time that both visiting team members and partners can get acquainted, such as a dinner meeting the evening before the visit. This encourages more spontaneity during the visit. Always call and confirm meeting date and objectives a few days in advance. (Refer to the Appendix for sample letters.)

Briefing packages and sessions

It is important that your team understand the purpose of the meeting and each member's role before the visit. (This also provides a contingency if someone is absent).

Review expectations during the briefing session to ensure that team members:

- Concentrate on learning if your benchmarking partner is doing something better and finding out why and how.
- Focus on the specific goals defined for the benchmarking project.

Two effective ways of doing this are to prepare a briefing package and conduct a briefing session a day or two before the visit to review preparations. If your team is new to benchmarking, you may wish to provide specific guidelines and some practice on interviewing techniques.

Develop a briefing package for all the attendees from your company using the information collected in Step 3 as a foundation. This should be provided to the attendees one or two days in advance so that the information is fresh. Depending on relevance, include such things as:

- Travel details and logistics.
  - Time, place, location, and purpose of meeting.
  - Contact information (lodging and company).
  - Attendees from both companies.
  - Ground transportation.
  - Other meeting locations.
- Company information.
  - Company overview.
  - Annual report.
  - Business articles.
  - Excerpts from previous visit reports.
- Meeting materials.
  - Agenda.
  - Question set.
  - Visiting tips.

Visit participants

The team participating in the visit typically consists of two to five people. Regardless of the number of attendees, be sure to assign:

- A leader responsible for asking questions. (If the question set is large and varied, this role may be split among team members.)
- A facilitator to ensure major points are addressed and to keep the meeting on track.
- A recorder (or scribe) to document the answers and edit the visit report. If the team is large, assign multiple recorders to help ensure accuracy.

These roles may change for specific topics. Although a person can have multiple roles, it is preferable to have one person assigned to each role.

Visit reports

A visit report provides a record of the visit and is useful to both the benchmarking team and other members of your corporation who may be interested in the subject matter discussed during the visit. Reports should be documented to ensure comprehensive coverage of all topics discussed. Hold a consensus meeting immediately after the visit with all participants to capture each person's perception of what occurred. Attendance of the entire group ensures objective documentation of the visit.

Bear in mind that writing the report may take anywhere from 4 to 30 person hours depending on the complexity and detail of the subject matter. In addition, send a final copy of the report to your sales account manager along with the list of attendees from both companies.

Make the report available to other organizations in your company that may find it useful unless legal obligations prohibit it. If you have a central library or database resource for benchmarking information, supply it with an abstract or the entire report.

Follow-up tips

Upon your return from the visit, remember to follow through with the hosting company by sending any materials that you promised to provide, along with a note thanking their participants for their time. Consider sending a preliminary copy of the visit report for their review to ensure accuracy. Keep the door open for asking additional questions and clarifying information.

Checkpoint

Before starting the next step, the benchmarking team should:

- Coordinate and communicate logistics for participation in applicable company visits.
- Communicate preliminary findings with stakeholders to maintain momentum as everyone awaits results.

Assessment

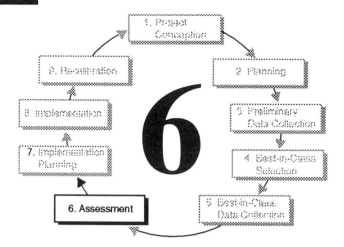

1. Project Conception
8. Recalibration
2. Planning
3. Implementation
3. Preliminary Data Collection
7. Implementation Planning
4. Best-in-Class Selection
5. Best-in-Class Data Collection
6. Assessment

The important thing in science is not so much to obtain new facts as to discover new ways of thinking about them.

Sir William Bragg

Activities in Step 6

Step 6 outlines the activities that help you:

- Use performance data to make relevant comparisons.
- Identify performance gaps (positive or negative) between your process and processes of potential best-in-class companies and determine why they exist.
- Identify areas where you are best-in-class.
- Understand how you can further benefit from the strengths of your process.
- Identify areas where other companies have best-in-class processes and understand why they are better than your processes.
- Understand how you can apply the superior practices of other companies to improve your process.
- Understand customer requirements compared to best-in-class.
- Develop recommendations, including goals and strategies.

Inputs

To begin the assessment step, you should have:

- Customer requirements.
- A current process description.
- Best-in-class process information.

Approach to Assessment

Reviewing performance measures

In this step, the benchmarking team looks at performance measurements and the process and environmental characteristics that underlie them. Performance measures are important to develop effective comparisons among products, services, and companies. They are driven by critical success factors and core competencies.

It usually takes a benchmarking team two to three weeks to complete analysis of the data obtained in the benchmarking effort. There are three phases of assessment:

1. Document comparable performance measures and process attributes.

   ■ Organizing information.

   ■ "Normalizing" data for relevant comparisons.

   ■ Comparing information.

2. Document findings.

   ■ Identify gaps.

   ■ Establish reasons for gaps.

   ■ Identify best practices and enablers for improvement.

3. Develop recommendations.

   ■ Project future performance.

   ■ Determine level of improvement needed.

   ■ Recommend goals, strategies, and performance targets for the future vision.

Sample comparison matrix

Organize the information you have obtained about your own and other processes into a format that enables you to compare performance measures and different process attributes. The following matrix provides one approach to presenting this information.

Attributes/ Measures	Process A	Process B	Process C	Own Process
Environment/ culture	▪ traditional ▪ established values ▪ espirit d'corp	▪ entrepreneurial ▪ guiding principles ▪ close-knit	▪ combo new/old ▪ values defined ▪ free-wheeling	▪ changing ▪ values not lived ▪ authoritarian
Structure	▪ functional ▪ flat	▪ flat ▪ autonomous	▪ flattened ▪ central planning	▪ away from hierarchical ▪ some autonomy
Cycle time	▪ 24 hrs ▪ 5% exceptions ▪ design teams	▪ 36 hrs ▪ 15% exceptions ▪ semi-automated	▪ 24 hours ▪ 3% exceptions ▪ highly automated	▪ 4 weeks ▪ 45% exceptions ▪ a few design teams
Defect rate	▪ .01	▪ .10	▪ .01	▪ .25
Training	▪ highly trained ▪ 80 hours/year	▪ some training ▪ 16 hours/year	▪ some training ▪ 25 hours/year	▪ some training ▪ 40 hours/year
Profitability	▪ sustained	▪ fluctuating	▪ sustained	▪ sustained
Service attributes	▪ 99% satisfied ▪ sustained service	▪ 75% satisfied ▪ too many errors	▪ 95% satisfied ▪ fluctuation	▪ 90% satisfied ▪ quality image

By reexamining your performance measures in comparison to best-in-class, you can determine the ones that have merit and are comparable. To do this successfully, you must consider your customers' needs, critical success factors, and internal process information.

If performance measures are not comparable, normalize performance data so you can make accurate assessments. Complexity factors are often used to normalize performance data on a ratio basis to avoid "apples to oranges" comparisons.

Document findings

Identify existing gaps in the data. Understand how far ahead your competitors and best-in-class companies are and determine the pace of change.

Consider factors that may contribute to these gaps. Use the Xerox approach[13] to focus on comparing:

▪ The goals that each company is trying to achieve.

▪ The fundamental practices that are part of the strategy to achieve these goals.

- The enablers, or piece parts, that comprise practices.
- Constraints.

Sample findings

The following sample assessment report for findings is based on the attributes presented in the sample comparison matrix.

- Values and guiding principles exist and are adhered to.
- Cycle time is between 24 and 36 hours.
- Defect rate is .01 for the best.
- Exceptions range from 3 percent to 15 percent of workload.
- Training is stressed and ranges from 25 hours to 80 hours per year.
- Customer satisfaction range is 95 percent to 99 percent but drops to 75 percent when too many errors are encountered.

Develop recommendations

Use performance measures and required trends to project future best-in-class performance levels.

Determine your own potential process capability and the degree of improvement needed to reach best-in-class performance in a specified period of time. Identify areas where substantial process change is required to achieve best-in-class performance. If the improvements needed are significant or radical, strategies might include business process re-engineering, corporate restructuring, or other radical changes. If improvement capabilities exist within the current process, include a quality improvement team, a new, more focused benchmarking effort, or implementation teams as part of your strategy.

Recommend new goals, performance targets, and strategies consistent with projected best performance.

Sample recommendations

The following sample assessment report for recommendations is based on the attributes presented in the sample comparison matrix.

- Critical
  - Cycle time reduction to 24 hours or less.
  - Defect rate reduced to .01 or less.
- Important
  - Values must be lived.
  - Active communication of values.

— Increased use of design teams.

■ Nice to Do

— Increase training to 80 hours per year.

— Continue drive to reduce hierarchy.

■ Not Relevant

— Style is not as important as sustained belief in values.

Checkpoint Before starting the next step, the team should:

■ Communicate findings and recommendations for incremental and breakthrough improvements to stakeholders (include costs, benefits, and preliminary action plans).

■ Refine recommendations based on feedback and get approval.

■ Develop supporting goals and strategies that are consistent with the organization's goals and strategies.

Implementation Planning

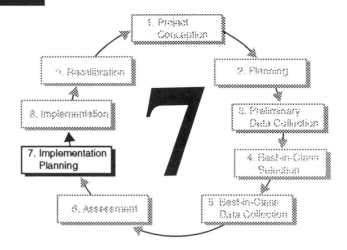

To live is to change and to be perfect is to be changed often.

John H. Newman

Activities in Step 7

If the benchmarking activity has been conducted within the context of process management, the process management team should now take responsibility for identifying improvement opportunities and driving those improvements to operational plans and recalibration plans.

Step 7 outlines the activities that help you:

- Assess the organization's readiness to change.

- Develop operational plans specific to the new process.

- Develop organizational change strategies.

- Develop implementation plans that help set the operational plans in place.

Inputs   To begin implementation planning, you should have:

- Goals and strategies for operational plans.
- Approved recommendations for improvement.

Creating the Vision of the Future

Description
The goals, strategies, and performance targets recommended in the previous step are now used to build a vision of what the organization will be like in the future and to plan for implementing the vision. The benchmarking team, process owner, senior management, sponsor, and other stakeholders participate in these activities.

The planning activities in this step produce two types of plans:

- Operational plans describe how the new organization or process will work.

- Implementation plans describe how the business will put the operational plans in place. They can be thought of as transition plans.

Assessing the readiness to change
The organization must evaluate its readiness to change before preparing operational and implementation plans. Receptiveness to the new vision and plan is based on:

- Degree of participation of process owners, customers, and stakeholders.

- Effectiveness of communication to stakeholders by the benchmarking team.

If participation and communication have been limited, stakeholders may offer resistance to change. In this case, the benchmarking team will need to launch a concerted effort to communicate their activities, findings, and new vision in order to enable and motivate change.

Developing operational plans
Operational plans provide the details of the future vision of the organization. The benchmarking team and process team should develop these operational plans and obtain stakeholder agreements and commitment. If a new process has been recommended, a new process owner may have to be identified.

Operational plans include:

- Vision statement.

- Future vision.

- New/refined practices.

- New/refined accountabilities, responsibilities, and customer/supplier relationships.

- New/refined measures and targets.

- New/refined reward systems.

- New/refined human resource policies and systems.

- Other operational details that help define the future vision.

Developing change strategies

The operational plans, the level of change, the size of the gap, and the time needed for change, help to determine whether to improve incrementally (process improvement) or make radical changes through reengineering. Radical changes may be evaluated on a trial basis using a pilot program.

To ease the transition, develop a strategy to manage that change. The strategy should include activities for:

- Integrating the changes into your organization's significant business processes such as planning, management, quality, finances, human resources, and reward systems.

- Ensuring changes are consistent with the new vision.

- Determining forces that may affect the implementation of the changes and developing ways to overcome negative forces.

- Incorporating action steps that serve as the driving forces for change into the implementation plans.

Developing implementation plans

Implementation plans provide the details, the roadmap, for moving the organization from the current state to the future vision. The implementation team should develop the implementation plans.

Identify a leader

As in any project, it is necessary to identify those involved and gain their support. Many of the same customers and stakeholders that were involved in the benchmarking project may also be involved in the implementation. Identify the implementation team leader. The implementation leader may be the process owner.

Roles and responsibilities

Clearly outline the implementation team's role and responsibilities. Obtain specific agreements regarding the level of support the implementation team expects to receive from the organization.

An implementation team should develop and execute the implementation plans and set up parameters to encourage change. Carefully consider who to include on the implementation team. At minimum, the implementation team should include the process owner, a benchmarking team representative, and key stakeholders. Limit the core team to a manageable set of five to eight people. Establish additional sub-teams if the magnitude of the change warrants it.

Early in the benchmarking process, the benchmarking team negotiated with the process owner to ensure adequate commitment to drive the benchmarking findings to operational plans and to provide the resources necessary for implementation. The benchmarking team must also agree to support these teams in their implementation planning by representing the benchmarking findings and assessment as required.

Elements of the implemen–tation plan

The implementation plan includes planning details for:

- Scope of the implementation effort.

- Strategies, goals, and objectives.

- Definitions and deliverables.

- Resources required and available (time, funding, training, and team).

- New methods and procedures that must be developed.

- Selecting beta or pilot sites.

- Milestones and tracking progress.

- Training schedules for management and operations on the improved process and any new systems.

- Communication strategy for stakeholders.

- New tools and skill requirements.

- New (in-house or out-sourced) development of software systems, training classes, and other new systems.

- Support structures necessary to equip people with the tools, skills, and systems needed to ensure their success.

- Progress and performance reports to check that the new process is in place and working.

- New measurements, standards, and objectives.

- A plan for recognizing both individuals and teams for implementing its changes.

- Final cut-over from the current process to the new process.

- A time frame for assessing gains once the new vision is realized.

- Contingency plans.

Checkpoint   Before starting the next step, ensure that:

- The benchmarking team and process owner work with senior management and other stakeholders to review benchmarking findings and determine the future vision.

- The future vision is articulated by senior management, sponsor, and champions and is incorporated within the strategic direction.

- The benchmarking team and process owner obtain approval for operational plans and implementation plans.

Implementation

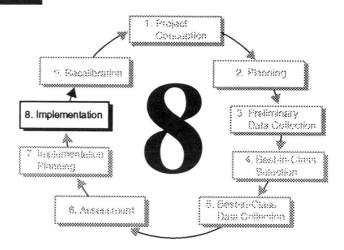

The Wright brothers flew right through the smoke screen of impossibility.

Charles F. Kettering

Activities in Step 8

Step 8 outlines the activities that help you:

- Understand what factors are critical to successful implementation.
- Organize, monitor, and control the progress of the implementation activities.
- Understand how to formalize, evaluate, and reach closure in the new future vision.

Inputs   To begin the implementation step, you should have:

- Operational plans that describe how the new process will work.
- Implementation plans to set the new process in place.

Ensuring Successful Implementation

Monitoring progress and refining plans

The implementation team must continually communicate and assess progress toward the future vision to stakeholders. To achieve this, progress reports should be completed frequently to:

- Communicate progress to date.

- Communicate performance and measures.

- Forecast milestones (activities and deliverables).

- Indicate planned deliverables.

- Document implementation changes to plan, concerns, issues, and jeopardies.

Share progress reports with all team members and stakeholders.

Encourage the sponsor and champions to frequently reinforce the future vision. Apprise the sponsor and champion of the status and potential problems through one-to-one communication in addition to the progress reports. Assist and encourage them in identifying and rewarding appropriate behavior and improved organizational performance.

Progress and performance reports serve as a basis for evaluating the efficiency and effectiveness of the operational and detailed implementation plans.

Based on this evaluation, refinements to the plans may be warranted. When conducted periodically and consistently, this evaluation and refinement allows course corrections as the team moves the organization toward its future vision. This avoids having the organization discover problems in the plans after it is too late to counteract them. Consistent with quality improvement, this helps the implementation team and stakeholders understand how the plan is actually working and the performance necessary to monitor improvements.

Managing change

Be prepared to adjust the implementation plan as a result of the organization's resistance to change. People who were initially enthusiastic may suddenly realize the magnitude of changes required and their enthusiasm may wane. The team must recognize the need for flexibility in both the schedule and design. Understand the reasons for resistance and address them as appropriate. Additional training, listening, coaching, and nurturing may be required before proceeding further with the plans. For more detail on implementation and managing change, refer to *Process Quality Management and Improvement*[14] and *The Reengineering Handbook.*[15]

Recognizing individuals and teams

Acknowledgment and support of individuals, teams, and overall organizational accomplishments creates a sense of progress, enthusiasm, and support for the transition to the future vision. Recognize those who demonstrate quality behaviors and values that contribute to that transition.

While change is often exciting and exhilarating, it can also be slow and frustrating. Without adequate support and recognition, the people involved may lose momentum. A recognition program helps offset the resistance to change. High-performing organizations inevitably convey the pride, admiration, and respect for accomplishments to those who are deserving. Remember *people* make things happen!

Closure

The implementation team should have established a milestone to signify when the organization reaches the future vision and is operating within the context of the new operational plans, to assess the gains. This is an ideal point to celebrate the successful accomplishment of the plans.

Checkpoint

Before moving on to the next step:

- Communicate progress, measures, and results with stakeholders.

- Ensure progress by revising implementation plans when necessary.

Recalibration

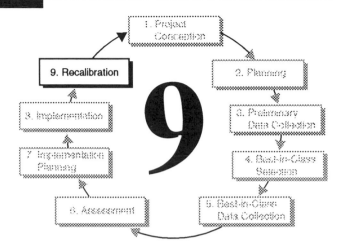

What we have to do is to be forever curiously testing new opinions and courting new impressions.

Walter Pater

Activities in Step 9

In the recalibration step, the benchmarking team checks and adjusts the benchmarking findings through an assessment of improvements made in the business process that was benchmarked. This reassessment determines the extent of any additional benchmarking activity that is required, how in-depth that activity should be, and at what intervals it should be conducted.

Step 9 outlines the activities that help you:

- Understand why recalibration is necessary.
- Know who should be involved in recalibration.
- Know how to perform recalibration.
- Develop a recalibration plan.

Inputs

To begin the recalibration step, you should:

- Know current business process performance levels.

- Know current customer satisfaction levels.

- Stay informed about ongoing secondary research on industry trends and developments.

Measuring Improvements

Approaching recalibration

Recalibration anticipates a dynamic industry, a competitive environment, and new innovations. Moreover, it supports continuous process improvement. Using recalibration to integrate future benchmarking activities into the business planning processes of the organization is a method of ensuring that benchmarking becomes a cyclical process within the framework of your business. The sponsor should assign the recalibration activity to the benchmarking team.

The purpose of recalibration is to ensure that improvements made to your process are bringing you closer to best-in-class performance. Have the benchmarking recommendations been incorporated, and how successful have they been? Have the changes positively impacted the root cause of process problems, customer satisfaction, and overall performance? To what degree has the industry improved its performance over the same interval?

Triggering recalibration

Consider what characteristics or measures should trigger recalibration. Triggers may include:

- Specific experiences arising from implementation efforts.
- Specific performance metrics and levels.
- Specific customer satisfaction metrics and levels.
- Competitor moves.
- New innovations or practices.
- A specific date or period of time.
- Critical external events.
- Process improvement opportunities.

Set up a plan to generate these triggers.

Recalibration activities may include:

- A full-fledged renewal of the benchmarking cycle.
- A planned and prepared visit to a newly identified company with an emerging best-in-class practice.

- Secondary research on an innovative process improvement.
- A breakthrough-thinking session.

Roles and responsi-bilities

Roles and responsibilities depend upon the trigger and the level of benchmarking activity it generates. Here are several examples:

- The process is dynamic, the environment is very competitive and the process has been identified as a critical customer satisfier.

  Triggers are established based on time, the level of customer satisfaction, and performance levels. These triggers specify several levels of activity: secondary research, breakthrough-thinking sessions, selected visits, or a renewed benchmarking project. Since this is a very critical process, a person might be assigned on a dedicated basis to monitor it.

- The process is less dynamic, but critical to the business.

  An annual time period trigger might be established to consider full renewal of the benchmarking project. A quarterly time period trigger might also be established to scan the environment for any new developments. The results of this quarterly secondary research may instigate the cycle earlier than annually if necessary. Someone may be assigned part-time to conduct the quarterly research. A benchmarking leader would be assigned at the time the full benchmarking cycle is performed anew.

- Improvements have been made to stabilize a process that was previously in danger.

  The team may elect, in this case, to use an emerging best-in-class practice and a six-month time period as triggers. The team may conduct a scan using secondary research every six months. If an emerging best practice is found, this would trigger a visit to the newly identified company with an emerging best-in-class practice to supplement the benchmarking findings. Responsibility for monitoring these triggers may be be assigned to the process owner.

Checkpoint

Once you have developed a recalibration plan, you should share the plan with all stakeholders and obtain their approval. This plan serves as a catalyst for the renewal of the benchmarking process and is integrated with the business planning process of the organization.

Appendix

This appendix provides additional information to help your team through the benchmarking effort. It includes:

- Ethical and competitive guidelines.
- A listing of recommended training and skills.
- A listing of suggested tools and techniques.
- A pre-visit checklist.
- Visiting tips.
- A post-visit checklist.
- An international protocol sample.
- Benchmarking case studies.
- A project plan sample.
- Sample topic areas and a preliminary question set.
- Sample request letter.

- Sample confirmation letter.
- Sample visit schedule.
- Sample thank-you letter.
- Visit report template.

Ethical and Competitive Guidelines

Bench–marking guidelines

"A complicated set of laws apply to the work that competitive intelligence (also benchmarking) professionals perform, however, virtually all of these rules derive from a fundamental commandment: *thou shalt not steal* - either from

- your competitors,
- your customers, or
- your own company.

This principle is embodied in more than three sets of laws, including: misappropriation of trade secrets, antitrust and insider trading."[16]

Critically assess your approach to benchmarking, with the following in mind:

- Never ask information from a benchmarking partner that you could or would not provide yourself;

- Never share information with competitors relating to pricing, costs, discounts, credit mark-ups, terms of sale, production levels or capacities, inventories, proposed new products/services, market plans or distribution arrangements with competitors, bidding choice of customers or sales territories, allocation of customers or sales territories, procurement arrangements, or salaries;

- During question set development, design questions so as not to lead into potentially proprietary areas;

- Defer to legal council associated within your corporation or individual business unit since legal positions on information sharing may vary;

- Before the visit, review rules associated with proprietary information with the team.

A set of basic legal principles, competitive guidelines and ethical standards should safeguard you from inappropriately approaching a benchmarking partner.

Refer to the following, or similar, sources before you approach external companies:

- AT&T. *Competition Guidelines.* Indianapolis: AT&T Customer Information Center. Select code 500-343.

- *AT&T Practices for Managing Intellectual Property.* (proprietary to AT&T)

- *AT&T Code of Conduct.* (proprietary to AT&T)

- Whalen and Hunger. 1991. *Strategic Management.* Third Edition. Indianapolis: AT&T Customer Information Center. Select code 0-201-50835-7.

- Manley II, Walter W. and William A. Shrode. 1990. *Critical Issues in Business Conduct: Legal and Social Challenges for the 1990s.* New York: Quorum Books.

- *The Benchmarking Code of Conduct.* 1992. The Council on Benchmarking of The Strategic Planning Institute and The International Benchmarking Clearinghouse, a service of The American Productivity and Quality Center.

Recommended Training and Skills

The following chart outlines the training and skills recommended for each step of the benchmarking process. For more information on the courses listed below, call 1-800-TRAINER.

Training and Skills	Part I	1	2	3	4	5	6	7	8	9
Benchmarking Techniques Workshop (CQ 1016)		■	■							
Benchmarking Sponsor Overview (CQ 1017)	■	■								■
Introduction to Project Management (MS 6310)		■	■					■	■	
Team Leader Training (CQ 1012)		■	■					■	■	■
Managing and Improving Processes with Quality (CQ 1004)		■		■						
Survey Design				■		■				
Interview Techniques (CD 4000)						■				
AT&T Technical Relations Center "Knowledge is Power" (videotape)						■				
Intro to News and Graphical Methods for Data Analysis (QU 1220)							■			
Data Collection, Analysis & Problem Solving (QS 2000)				■			■			
Effective Customer Satisfaction (PS 4000)	■	■						■	■	■
High Gain Listening (MS 6331)				■		■				
Influence: Collaborating for Results (MD 7750)							■			
Process Quality Management & Improvement (QS 1900)	■	■	■					■		

Suggested Tools and Techniques

The following chart lists the tools and techniques that you may find useful throughout the steps of the benchmarking process.

Tools and Techniques	Step								
	1	2	3	4	5	6	7	8	9
Affinity Diagrams	■	■	■			■	■		
Activity Network Diagram		■					■		
Brainstorming	■	■	■				■	■	■
Cause and Effect (Ishikawa)	■	■				■	■	■	
Control Charts						■	■	■	
Facilitator Guide/Interview Techniques	■	■	■		■	■	■		
Flowcharts	■	■	■			■			
Force Field Analysis	■	■				■	■		
Interrelationship Digraph						■	■		■
Matrix Diagram	■	■	■	■		■	■		■
Multivoting	■	■		■			■		
Pareto Diagrams		■				■	■		
Post-Visit Checklist					■				
Pre-Visit Checklist				■	■				
Prioritization Matrices		■		■			■		
Process Decision Program Chart (PDPC)		■					■		
Process Quality Management & Improvement (PQMI)	■	■	■			■	■	■	■
Project Management Tools		■	■	■	■	■	■	■	■
Project Plan	■	■	■	■	■	■	■	■	■
Quality Function Deployment		■		■		■	■		
Selection Matrix			■	■					
Timeline		■					■		
Tree Diagram		■		■		■	■		
Visiting Tips				■	■				
Xerox's "Z-Chart"						■			

References   For detailed information on the tools and techniques listed in the chart, consult:

- Brassard, Michael. 1989. *Memory Jogger Plus+™: Featuring the Seven Management and Planning Tools.* Methuen, MA: GOAL/QPC.

- King, Robert. 1989. *Hoshin Planning: The Developmental Approach.* Methuen, MA: GOAL/QPC Inc.

- AT&T Quality Steering Committee. 1988. *Process Quality Management & Improvement.* Indianapolis: AT&T Customer Information Center. Select code 500-049.

- Camp, Robert C. 1989. *Benchmarking—The Search for Industry Best Practices that Lead to Superior Performance.* Milwaukee, WI: ASQC Quality Press.

- AT&T Quality Steering Committee. 1990. *Analyzing Business Process Data: The Looking Glass.* Indianapolis: AT&T Customer Information center. Select code 500-445.

Pre-Visit Checklist

Company to be visited

- Hold initial discussions with legal, benchmarking interviewee.
- Send letter to confirm meeting (include question set, if possible).
- Call interviewee to confirm meeting and logistics.

Bench–marking team

- All involved understand the defined purpose of study.
- A set of objectives and questions have been agreed upon.
- Responsibilities are assigned for visit negotiations, correspondence, question set, briefing package, notetaking, and writing of visit report.
- The team can provide answers about its own operation, if asked, for each of the questions the team plans to ask.
- All attendees have received the briefing package.
- A pre-visit discussion has been held with all team attendees to confirm roles and finalize plans. (Note that a minimum of one person should be assigned to each of the roles: interviewer, documenter/observer, and facilitator).
- The benchmarking team has been kept apprised of visit status.

Visiting Tips

General tips

- Be professional, honest, courteous, and prompt.
- Use universal language instead of company jargon.
- If you do not receive the answer you expect, try rephrasing the question to be sure both parties understand it.

Beginning of visit

- Introduce all attendees and explain why they are present.
- Clearly state the objectives and process.
- Mention that you have selected them because they have done a superior job and indicate your source.
- Begin questioning with general areas of interest or open-ended questions first. Follow these with specific questions.

During visit

- Focus on information critical to primary objectives.
- Remember, only one member should ask questions at a time and only one question should be asked at a time.
- Be sure neither party is sharing proprietary information unless prior approval has been obtained by both parties.
- Never share information with competitors about pricing, costs, discounts, credit, mark-up, terms of sale, production levels or capacities, inventories, products and services (proposed, new, or existing), market plans, distribution arrangements, bidding, choice of customers or sales territories, allocation of customers or sales territories, procurement arrangements, or salaries.

Visit wrap-up

- Offer to share your general findings.
- Set the stage for further benchmarking in the future.

Post-Visit Checklist

- Allow time to debrief immediately after the visit.
- Send a thank-you letter to the host.
- Write visit report using a consistent format across visits.
- Provide a copy of visit report to all participants.
- Incorporate results with other visit results.

International Protocol Checklist

**Understand-
ing cultural
differences**

In benchmarking, as in other international negotiations, you must understand the cultural differences that may exist when selecting benchmarking partners outside the United States. Before approaching potential benchmarking partner, research their country and culture to avoid misunderstandings and unrealistic expectations. Consider the following[17,18] when benchmarking internationally:

- Does the country have a special benchmarking or business etiquette?

- How formally do they conduct business? How much time would they prefer to spend getting to know each other before reaching agreement?

- Does your business have existing relationships with the company in that country? Would those in your company with an existing relationship be willing to provide a letter of introduction to the potential benchmarking partner?

- Who should introduce you to the potential benchmarking partner?

- Has a foundation of trust been established?

- Who will make the final decision to agree to benchmark with you?

- What are your goals and objectives? Do you understand their objectives?

- What type of personal relationship is expected?

- Are commitments made verbally or in writing?

- Have you verified your commitment?

- How important is the use of business cards? Should they be printed in the host's native language? When and how are they shared?

- Is it acceptable to refer to each other on a first name basis?

- What language will the visit be conducted in?

- What degree of "small talk" is acceptable?

- Refusing to accept a beverage or other hospitality in some countries is considered an insult. Is that the case with the country you plan to visit?

- Do you know at least a few words in the language of your benchmarking partner?

- Is a handshake or bow appropriate upon meeting face-to-face?

- Does the country consider time differently, such as promptness versus lateness for meetings?

- If you plan to have a meal with the benchmarking partner, is it appropriate to discuss business while eating or to have a toast beforehand? What other dining rituals should you be aware of?

- What are the social mores of the country?

- What is the acceptable "spatial proximity" when standing next to each other? Is it considered an insult if you step back to increase the distance between each other?

- Although small gifts are appropriate in any business negotiation, are there gifts that are inappropriate or more desirable?

- Is gift-giving considered an important part of the culture?

AT&T Case Study: Direct Delivery Service

**Objective
of study**

To examine the Direct Delivery Service process and implement
improvements to reduce cost while improving quality.

**Description
of team**

Seven distribution team members and three cross-functional team
members.

Benefit

Benchmarking other companies indicated the importance of an integrated
process with mechanization in material handling through conveyorization.
The resulting conveyor-based picking system provided 99.7 percent
accuracy with one-year payback based on savings in:

- Carton forming.
- Carton supply.
- Material handling.
- Corrugated recycling.
- Dunnage and carton sealing.
- Ability to handle peak loads.

AT&T Case Study: Pollution Prevention Program

Objective of study	To develop a corporate pollution prevention program based on best-in-class programs.
Description of team	Two corporations partnered to compare their current pollution prevention programs to the best-in-class and to build an improved program based on the best elements found in several programs.
	Members included: a senior manager, a manager responsible for developing a corporate pollution prevention program, a manager who had successfully implemented a pollution prevention program, a quality manager for the area requesting the benchmarking, a member from environmental research, and a benchmarking facilitator.
Benefit	The team identified the critical path for developing and maintaining a corporate-wide pollution prevention program. In addition, it adopted many of the conventions and practices that were working well in other companies.

AT&T Case Study: Recruiting and Hiring Process

Objective of study	To compare the recruiting and hiring process to best-in-class companies with a similar business unit structure.
Description of team	A co-located group of five human resources managers and an internal benchmarking consultant.
Benefit	The contracting process between corporate human resources and the business unit and divisional customers was not working. Customers, in some cases, were providing part of the recruiting and hiring service themselves, yet paying a one-price contract fee to the corporate organization.
	As a result, corporate human resources backed up their service with comparison of cost per hire data and offered customers the option of picking from a menu only those services they chose to purchase. The study was highly successful and other corporate organizations followed suit.

101

AT&T Case Study: R&D Management Process

Objective of study	To develop strategies for best managing R&D resources in support of distributed businesses and the long-term business strategy.
Description of team	R&D executives representing various business units and common technology organizations were responsible for developing strategies and were supported by a team of eight internal benchmarking consultants and one external benchmarking consultant. Specific areas of focus and benchmark companies were assigned to executive sub-teams, supported by individual benchmarking consultants. Analyses and recommendations were completed by the sub-teams and integrated by the consultants into a final report.
Benefit	The study contributed to several actions by the R&D community. Corporate R&D objectives were set to improve the rate of introduction of new products as well as the rate of introduction of new technology into new products. Chief technical officers were appointed to build associated strategies and plans, and to strengthen associated relationships with corporate research.

Benchmarking Project Plan - DATE

Developed by	XYZ Benchmarking Team.
Introduction	Identify the sponsoring organization and explain why the project was initiated.
Benchmark–ing process	Describe the benchmarking process that the team will use (i.e., The AT&T Benchmarking Process).
Key players	Identify process owner(s), sponsor, customer(s), supplier(s), benchmarking leader, benchmarking team members, and other stakeholders.
Scope	Describe the focus and boundaries of the project.
Objectives	State what the team intends to accomplish.
Deliverables	Describe the activities and milestones associated with each of the following:

- A project plan.
- Detailed process diagrams and flowcharts for your own business process.
- Performance metrics (baseline data).
- Secondary research.
- Best-in-class selection criteria and matrix.
- Best-in-class selections.
- Topic areas and question sets.
- Briefing packages.
- Visit reports.
- Assessment report (including gap analysis).
- Recommendations.

- Operational plans.
- Implementation plans.
- Progress reports.
- A recalibration plan.

Resources	Estimate the number of people, time, dollars, systems, equipment, and other support required and available.
Roles and responsibilities	Clearly state key players' responsibilities and accountabilities.
Performance metrics	Identify key metrics for data collection activities.
Communication process	Describe vehicles, frequency, and stakeholders for targeted communications throughout the project.
Contingency plans	Identify conceivable contingencies and develop plans to address them.
Maintenance	Indicate how this plan will be reviewed and updated throughout the project.

Timeline sample

In the timeline, indicate major activities and milestones. Also include a detailed list of milestones and responsibilities.

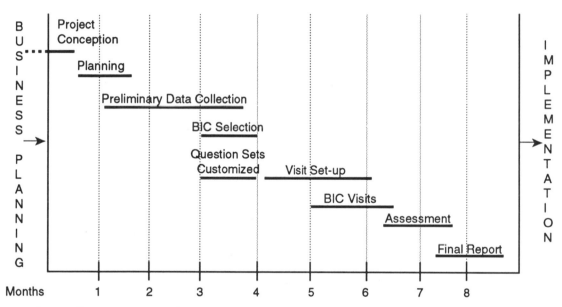

Assumptions:

1. Benchmarking Team (5-8 people)
2. Preliminary Data Collection (30 days for selected companies)
3. BIC Selection and Question Set Customization (2 days)
4. Visit Set-up per company (3 days)
5. BIC Visit per company (2 days)
6. Visit Report Write-up per visit (3 days)
7. Assessment (4 days)
8. Final Report (5 days)
9. Separate Implementation Team

Sample Topic Areas and Preliminary Question Set

This is a sample of topic areas and a question set that a small entrepreneurial firm might use when benchmarking to improve its deployment of best practices in each area of its business.

I. Background

    A. Describe the overall philosophy of your organization.

    B. Describe the general structure of your organization.

    C. How many years has your benchmarking program been in existence?

    D. How many best practices have you identified?

II. Best Practices Program Development

    A. How was the concept for the program developed?

    B. How were customer needs determined?

    C. How were roles and responsibilities determined and agreed upon?

    D. How long did it take to establish the program from the concept to the first best practice use in the organization?

III. Best Practices Deployment Process

    A. How are best practices identified?

    B. How are best practices agreed upon?

    C. How are best practices deployed?

    D. Who is involved in the deployment process?

    E. What are the strengths of the program?

    F. Are there any areas targeted for improvement?

IV. Measurement System

    A. How many best practices have you identified?

    B. How do you assess the impact of best practices on your customers' satisfaction?

    C. What other critical factors contribute to the success of best practices being deployed?

    D. What metrics do you use to evaluate the effectiveness of your best practices?

    E. What metrics do you use to evaluate the effectiveness and efficiency of the successful deployment of your best practices?

V. Reward and Recognition System

    A. What type of reward and recognition system do you have in place to recognize teams and individuals who follow identified best practices?

Sample Request Letter

DATE

BIC Corporation Contact
BIC Corporation
Street Address
City, State Zip

Corporation Contact:

I enjoyed our telephone conversation on (date). Per our discussion, our ABC organization is improving its XYZ process through benchmarking others who are best-in-class. Your corporation often receives recognition for excellence in this area, especially, your recent award in customer satisfaction by *Customer World, Inc.*

We would like to arrange a meeting with you within the next two months to discuss in detail aspects of your XYZ process. Attached is a brief overview of our organization and the topic areas we plan to address during the exchange.

Based on your agreement, four or five people will attend the session. Among the attendees will be a director and two managers from the XYZ area, as well as our internal benchmarking consultant.

If you have any questions, please call me at (telephone number).

Sincerely,

Benchmarking Leader

Sample Confirmation Letter

DATE

BIC Corporation Contact
BIC Corporation
Street Address
City, State Zip

Corporation Contact:

Thank you for agreeing to meet with our ABC organization to discuss your XYZ process. We have developed the attached question set to facilitate the exchange.

Attendees from our company will be:

- Name 1, director of the XYZ area

- Name 2, product manager of the XYZ area

- Name 3, line manager of the XYZ operation center

- Name 4, assistant product manager of the XYZ area

- Name 5, benchmarking consultant

We look forward to meeting with you on (date) from (time) at your headquarters office. We appreciate the invitation to lunch and we all plan to attend. We will forward our travel itinerary to you in advance of the meeting.

If you have any questions, please call me at (telephone number).

Sincerely,

Benchmarking Leader

Sample Visit Schedule

Company	Company A	Company B	Company C
Location	Cupertino, CA	Kyoto, Japan	Brussels, Belgium
Contact **Telephone**	Name A	Name B	Name C
Attendees			
Date			
Time			
Place			
Remarks			

Sample Thank-you Letter

DATE

BIC Corporation Contact
BIC Corporation
Street Address
City, State Zip

Corporation Contact:

Thank you for hosting our benchmarking meeting on (date). The information we discussed will be invaluable input into our XYZ process improvement plans. We especially thank Name 1, Name 2, Name 3, Name 4, and Name 5 for dedicating their time to share with us.

We look forward to a continuing benchmarking partnership with you. As mentioned at the meeting, do not hesitate to call us based on your interest in benchmarking the XYZII process.

Sincerely,

Benchmarking Leader

Visit Report Template

Date of Report

Project Number | If the benchmarking study has a specific identifier, place that here.

Study Description | Describe the purpose and objectives of the benchmarking study.

Involved Organizations | Identify what groups across the organization are involved in the benchmarking study.

Company Visited

Date Visited

Host Attendees | Identify names, titles, and functions.

Visiting Attendees | Identify names, titles, and functions.

Background | Provide general background about the company and why selected.

Key Findings | Highlight information that is particularly relevant and may be critical to the success of the company visited.

Details of Visit | Structure this section, which records details of the meeting, based upon the topic areas of your question set.

Glossary

A

activity network diagram

This tool is used to plan the most appropriate schedule for any complex task and all of its related subtasks. It projects likely completion time and monitors all subtasks for adherence to the necessary schedule. This is used when the task at hand is a familiar one with subtasks that are of a known duration.

This tool is useful during development of the benchmarking project plan (Step 2 of the AT&T Benchmarking Process). It may also be useful, in some aspects of implementation planning.

affinity diagram

A method used in a group setting to categorize different opinions, ideas, or problems. First, group members generate ideas and write each one on a card. Then, they sort the cards into categories and assign labels to each category of cards.

analogs

Processes that are sufficiently similar to enable comparisons.

assessment

A planned activity to measure the effectiveness of a process improvement or of an organization's quality system.

In benchmarking, this is the activity of measuring and comparing your own process with that of best-in-class processes.

assessment report

A document resulting from analysis of data gathered throughout the benchmarking effort indicating position relative to best-in-class.

awareness phase

The first of four phases of an organization's quality evolution (as described in the *Quality Manager's Handbook*).[19] In this phase, all employees become aware of the need for quality improvement. The beginning of the awareness phase is characterized by confusion, indirect communication, and a quality effectiveness score of 200 or less, as measured by the Baldrige Quality Award criteria.

B

benchmarking

A process for continuously measuring a company's current business operations and comparing them to best-in-class operations.

benchmarking leader

The individual who manages the benchmarking project.

benchmarking team

The group of individuals who collaborate in the benchmarking activity.

best-in-class

Receiving highest marks against comparable products, services, or processes when evaluated by a set of established criteria.

brainstorming

A group problem-solving technique that involves the spontaneous contribution of ideas from all members of the group.

briefing package

A synopsis of essential information on a particular company to prepare for a benchmarking visit.

C

cause and effect diagram

A graphic tool used to visually isolate an effect and to diagram possible related causes. Can be used to identify root causes of problems. Also known as a fishbone or Ishikawa diagram.

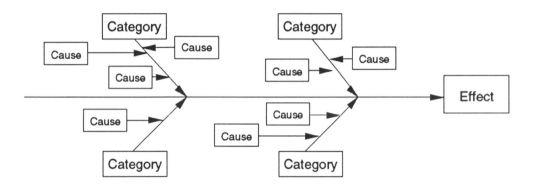

Chairman's Quality Award

A prestigious AT&T internal quality award that recognizes individual business unit and division leadership in quality. The criteria for the award are based on the criteria for the Malcolm Baldrige National Quality Award. The AT&T Corporate Quality Office administers the award.

champion

An individual who initially defends the benchmarking effort and helps remove impending obstacles.

competitive benchmarking

The process of measuring a company's current business operations against that of direct competitors. When conducting this type of benchmarking, a company must ensure compliance with strict competitive, ethical, legal, and intellectual property guidelines.

control chart

A graphic tool that plots samples over time to evaluate whether a process is statistically in control.

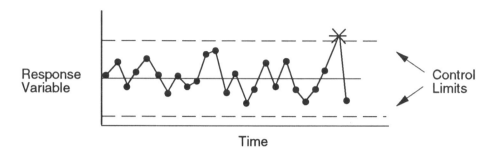

customer-supplier model

A representation of a work process that establishes relationships between customer and supplier, process input and process output, and requirements and feedback.

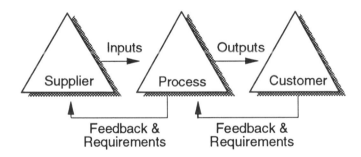

In benchmarking, this model is useful in the earlier steps as you examine process characteristics, define the scope, and focus on customer requirements.

F

flowchart
A pictorial representation of the steps in a process.

force field analysis
A method for identifying the driving and restraining forces that affect process performance. Normally used with a pictorial diagram showing driving forces pushing up on a horizontal line and restraining forces on the top pushing down. Removal of a restraining force or addition of another driving force causes the level of performance to improve.

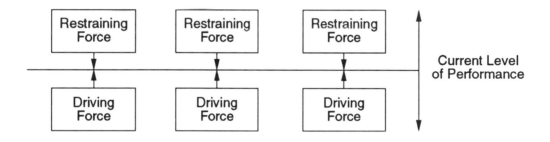

H

Hoshin planning
Hoshin planning is a planning system that allows a business to plan and execute strategic organizational breakthrough (policy deployment aspect the business planning process).

I

implementation plan
Describes how the business will put the operational plans in place.

Interrelationship Digraph
This tool takes complex, multi-variable problems or desired outcomes and explores and displays all of the interrelated factors involved. It graphically shows the logical (and often causal) relationships between factors.

It may be used to help create the future vision and develop operational and implementation plans; it may also be used to evaluate triggers during recalibration; (Steps 7 and 9 of the AT&T Benchmarking Process).

Ishikawa: cause and effect diagram
See *cause and effect diagram.*

K

knowledge phase
The second of four phases of an organization's quality evolution (as described in the *Quality Manager's Handbook*).[20] In this phase, all employees begin to obtain and apply basic quality knowledge and techniques. The knowledge phase begins with members of the organization communicating requirements to their suppliers and obtaining feedback from their customers. In a self-assessment of the organization's quality system effectiveness, managers give their organization a score of approximately 400, as measured by the Baldrige Quality Award criteria.

M

Malcolm Baldrige National Quality Award
An award recognizing United States businesses for quality leadership. The award is managed by the National Institute of Standards and Technology, U.S. Department of Commerce.

matrix diagram
This versatile tool shows the connection (or correlation) between each idea/issue in one group of items and each idea/issue in one or more other groups of items. At each intersecting point between a vertical set of items and horizontal set of items a relationship is indicated as being either present or absent. In its most common use the matrix diagram takes the necessary tasks (often from the tree diagram) and graphically displays their relationships with people, functions, or other tasks. This is frequently used to determine who has responsibility for the different parts of an implementation plan.

This tool is useful during planning (Steps 2 and 7 of the AT&T Benchmarking Process). It also may adapted for use as an alternative to the selection matrix in facilitating selection of best-in-class companies (Step 4 of the AT&T Benchmarking Process).

multivoting
A structured series of votes often used to help teams assign priorities in a list of many items and then reduce the list to a manageable few (usually three to five).

O

operational plan
Provides the details of the future vision of the organization. It describes how the new organization or process will work.

P

Pareto diagram

A graphic tool used to rank problems and opportunities by occurrence and other scales of importance.

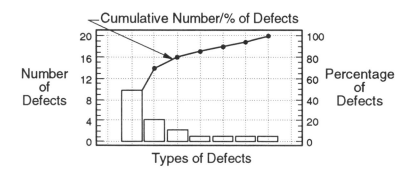

performance metrics

Measures that calibrate the effectiveness and efficiency of a process in meeting customer requirements.

prioritization matrices

These tools take tasks, issues, or possible actions and prioritize them based on known, weighted criteria. They utilize a combination of tree and matrix diagram techniques, thus narrowing down options to those that are the most desirable or effective.

These tools are useful during planning (Steps 2 and 7 of the AT&T Benchmarking Process). They also may adapted for use as an alternative to the selection matrix in facilitating selection of best-in-class companies (Step 4 of the AT&T Benchmarking Process).

Process Decision Program Chart (PDPC)

This tool maps out every conceivable event and contingency that can occur when moving from a problem statement to the possible solutions. This is used to plan each possible chain of events that needs to happen when the problem or goal is an unfamiliar one.

This tool is useful during planning for contingencies (Steps 2 and 7 of the AT&T Benchmarking Process).

process improvement
Activities aimed at establishing initial control; improving process performance with respect to customer needs, cost and timeliness; providing new sources of customer value; responding to changes in customer needs or market conditions; and holding the gains from improvement activities. Improvement covers incremental changes to the process as well as radical changes brought about through process reengineering.

process owner
The individual ultimately accountable and responsible for process performance. This person coordinates process management activities, has authority or ability to make changes in the process, and manages the process end-to-end to ensure optimal overall performance. The process owner is usually a higher-ranking manager than any member of the process team and may be a member of the business management team that charters the process management activity.

Process Quality Management and Improvement (PQMI)
A seven-step methodology for process management and continuous improvement outlined in the *Process Quality Management & Improvement Guidelines*.[21]

progress report
A document that communicates advancement towards a set of goals and objectives, and raises any jeopardies or schedule changes.

project management
The planning, organizing, directing, and controlling of company resources for a finite, often relatively short-term objective (a project) that has been established to complete specific goals. Typical project management tools include: project plans, the critical path method (CPM), PERT/GANTT charts, timelines, and cost-benefit analysis.

project plan
The detailed formulation of a program of action to accomplish desired goals and objectives.

Q

Quality Improvement Team (QIT)
A group charged with planning and implementing a quality improvement project. Teams consist of a team leader, a quality manager (consultant), and team members.

quality management

The management of a process or an entire business to maximize customer satisfaction at the lowest overall cost to the organization.

question set

A series of objective and structured inquiries used to collect data.

R

recalibration plan

A document that identifies triggers for benchmarking activities to ensure continual comparison of the business process against evolving best-in-class practices.

S

secondary research

Collecting information about a particular subject using existing information consultants and other secondary sources.

selection criteria

An important set of definitive and limiting characteristics or performance metrics used to select best-in-class processes for benchmarking.

selection matrix

This tool is similar to the matrix diagram. It shows the relationship between the selection criteria used to identify best-in-class processes and the identified best-in-class processes.

This tool is useful in facilitating identification and selection of best-in-class companies (Steps 3 and 4 of the AT&T Benchmarking Process).

sponsor

An individual that funds and assumes responsibility for the benchmarking effort and results.

stakeholders
> People who hold some share in the management responsibilities of a process. Stakeholders may include the process owner, process managers, key managers working in the process, and process management team members and their managers.

supplier
> Source of material and/or information for a process; may be internal or external to the company, organization, or group.

T

topic areas
> A set of subjects of interest that results in an outline for organizing data to be collected.

Total Quality Approach (TQA)
> A strategy for integrating quality practices and tools into the management of all phases of the business. AT&T's Total Quality Approach consists of four elements: customer focus, process management and improvement, supplier partnership, and leadership and involvement of people.

tree diagram
> This tool systematically maps out in increasing detail the full range of paths and tasks that need to be accomplished in order to achieve a primary goal and every related subgoal. Graphically, it resembles an organization chart or family tree.
>
> This tool may be used to develop the benchmarking project plan and implementation plans (Steps 2 and 7 of the AT&T Benchmarking Process).

V

visit reports
> A document that provides a record of the information exchange between two companies or organizations.

W

wisdom phase
The third of four phases of an organization's quality evolution (as described in the *Quality Manager's Handbook*[22]). In this phase, managers, employees, natural work groups, and functional organizations cooperate among themselves and partner with customers and suppliers. An external evaluation of the organization's quality system effectiveness results in a Baldrige Quality award score of approximately 600.

world-class
Ranking among the best across all comparable products, services, or processes (not just direct competitors) in terms of critical performance or features as perceived by customers and industry experts.

world-class phase
The fourth of four phases of an organization's quality evolution (as described in the *Quality Manager's Handbook*[23]). In this phase, customers and suppliers constantly team together to achieve mutual customer and business goals. An external evaluation of the organization's quality system effectiveness results in a Baldrige Quality Award score of 800 or better.

X

Xerox's Z-Chart
A graphic portrayal of the size of the existing performance gap between one's own process and that of best-in-class. It is broken down into three essential components: historical trend, current gap, and the projected future performance level necessary to achieve superior or competitive performance.

References

[1] U.S. Department of Commerce. 1992. *Award Criteria: Malcolm Baldrige National Quality Award.* Milwaukee: American Society for Quality Control. pp. 8.

[2] AT&T Quality Steering Committee. 1990. *Leading the Quality Initiative.* Indianapolis: AT&T Customer Information Center. Select code 500-441.

[3] King, Robert. 1989. *Hoshin Planning: The Developmental Approach.* Methuen, MA: GOAL/QPC Inc.

[4] Nadler, David A. and Michael L. Tushman. 1990. "Beyond the Charismatic Leader: Leadership and Organizational Change." *California Management Review.* (Winter), pp. 77-97.

[5] AT&T Quality Steering Committee. 1990. *Quality Manager's Handbook.* Indianapolis: AT&T Customer Information Center. Select code 500-442.

[6] AT&T Quality Steering Committee. 1988. *Process Quality Management and Improvement.* Indianapolis: AT&T Customer Information Center. Select code 500-049.

[7] Levine, Harvey A. 1986. *Project Management Using Microcomputers.* (Berkeley), CA: Osborne McGraw-Hill, p. 2.

[8] Brassard, Michael. 1989. *Memory Jogger Plus+^{TM}: Featuring the Seven Management and Planning Tools.* Methuen, MA: Goal/QPC.

[9] AT&T Quality Steering Committee. 1990. *The Quality Improvement Team Helper.* Indianapolis: AT&T Customer Information Center. Select code 500-444.

[10] Juran, J. M., F. M. Gryna, and R. S. Bingham. 1974. *Quality Control Handbook.* Third edition. New York: McGraw-Hill, Inc. pp. 2-17–2-18.

[11] Prahalad, C. K. and Gary Hamel. 1990. "The Core Competence of the Corporation." *Harvard Business Review.* (May/June), p. 82.

[12] Camp, Robert C. 1989. *Benchmarking—The Search for Industry Best Practices That Lead to Superior Performance.* Milwaukee, WI: ASQC Quality Press.

[13] Camp, Robert C. 1989. *Benchmarking—The Search for Industry Best Practices That Lead to Superior Performance.* Milwaukee, WI: ASQC Quality Press.

[14] AT&T Quality Steering Committee. 1990. *Quality Manager's Handbook.* Indianapolis: AT&T Customer Information Center. Select code 500-442.

[15] AT&T Quality Steering Committee. 1992. *The Reengineering Handbook.* Indianapolis: AT&T Customer Information Center. Select code 500-449.

[16] Smith II, Dwight C. "A Legal Perspective on the Ethics of Competitive Intelligence." 1989. *Competitive Intelligence.* Volume 4, Issue 2. pp. 1,13.

[17] Rossman, Marlene L. 1986. *The International Business Woman: A Guide to Success in the Global Marketplace."* New York: Praeger Publishers.

[18] Rowland, Diana. 1985. *Japanese Business Etiquette: A Practical Guide to Success with the Japanese."* New York: Warner Books.

[19] AT&T Quality Steering Committee. 1990. *Quality Manager's Handbook.* Indianapolis: AT&T Customer Information Center. Select code 500-442.

[20] AT&T Quality Steering Committee. 1990. *Quality Manager's Handbook.* Indianapolis: AT&T Customer Information Center. Select code 500-442.

[21] AT&T Quality Steering Committee. 1988. *Process Quality Management and Improvement.* Indianapolis: AT&T Customer Information Center. Select code 500-049.

[22] AT&T Quality Steering Committee. 1990. *Quality Manager's Handbook.* Indianapolis: AT&T Customer Information Center. Select code 500-442.

[23] AT&T Quality Steering Committee. 1990. *Quality Manager's Handbook.* Indianapolis: AT&T Customer Information Center. Select code 500-442.

126

Supporting the Total Quality Approach:
The AT&T Quality Library

AT&T's Total Quality Approach defines the fundamental building blocks from which the business units and divisions construct their quality systems. AT&T provides resources— including the AT&T Quality Library—to help organizations adapt and augment the elements of the Total Quality Approach to meet the expectations of their customers and the needs of their business. The books of the Quality Library are available through the AT&T Customer Information Center (1-800-432-6600).

Quality Technology and Tools Series

Design for Quality and Reliability Volume (500-178)

Quality by Design (500-021)
A quality manual for the AT&T R&D community.

Reliability by Design (010-810-105)
A reliability manual for the AT&T R&D community.

Data Quality Volume (500-487)

Data Quality Foundations (500-490)
Introduction to basic concepts and dimensions of data quality.

Describing Information Processes: The FIP Technique (500-488)
A complement to standard flowcharting, especially useful for understanding information processes.

Improving Data Accuracy: The Data Tracking Technique (500-489)
A proven method to improve data accuracy.

Tools for Quality Management Volume (500-455)

Analyzing Business Process Data: The Looking Glass (500-445)
Help on using statistical quality control techniques to understand, control, and improve business processes.

AT&T Cost-of-Quality Guidelines (500-746)
Suggestions for estimating costs of appraisal, prevention, and corrective action and for using the data to select improvement opportunities.

AT&T Statistical Quality Control Handbook (700-444)
The classical text that has taught statistical process control to thousands worldwide.

Benchmarking: Focus on World-Class Practices (500-454)
AT&T's approach to identifying and adapting world-class practices for business and process improvement.

Quality Management and Systems Series

People, Leadership, and Involvement Volume (500-456)

AT&T's Total Quality Approach (500-452)
An overview of the quality principles and practices that underlie how AT&T manages its business to meet the needs of customers, employees, stockholders, and communities.

Batting 1000: Using Baldrige Feedback to Improve Your Business (500-451)
A strategy for using feedback from the Baldrige Award evaluation process to improve your business.

Leading the Quality Initiative (500-441)
Eight action areas that define a Quality Council's role in adapting and implementing AT&T's Total Quality Approach.

Policy Deployment (500-453)
A reference to help managers achieve break-through improvements in business capabilities by aligning improvement efforts with strategic goals to meet customer and business needs.

Quality Manager's Handbook (500-442)
A road map for the quality manager with recommended tools, references, and re-sources for building a world-class quality system.

Process Management and Improvement Volume (500-457)

AT&T Quality Improvement Cycle (500-031)
An eight-step approach to problem-solving and quality improvement.

Process Quality Management and Improvement Guidelines (PQMI) (500-049)
A customer-focused, seven-step cycle for management, control, and improvement of business processes.

PQMI: Tips, Experiences, and Lessons Learned (500-446)
Practical advice and examples based on AT&T experience for applying PQMI and other process management methodologies.

Quality Improvement Team Helper (500-444)
Guidelines for starting a quality improvement team.

Reengineering Handbook (500-449)
Approach to redesigning a process to make substantial improvement in meeting customer requirements and increasing efficiency.

Customer Focus Volume (500-458)

Achieving Customer Satisfaction (500-443)
A strategy for using customer and competitor information to increase customer satisfaction.

Great Performances! The Best in Customer Satisfaction and Customer Service (500-450)
A look at how world-class companies make customer satisfaction a total business strategy.

Reference Series

A History of Quality Control and Assurance at AT&T: 1920-1970
(500-721, booklet and 14 videotapes; 500-722, booklet only)
Videotaped interviews with AT&T people and their colleagues whose work advanced the development and application of quality methods.

AT&T Quality Glossary (500-745)
Definitions of terms and acronyms.

For AT&T employees only:
AT&T Quality Management Contacts Directory (500-454)
AT&T Quality Resources Directory (500-298)